Ex Libris

Deirdre Kumpfbeck

Training the Horse and Rider

Mrs. Liselott Linsenhof on *Piaff* (West Germany). *(Photograph by Lichtbildstelle BMfluF.)*

A Book of Dressage

Training the Horse and Rider

Fritz Stecken

ARCO PUBLISHING COMPANY INC.

219 Park Avenue South, New York, N.Y. 10003

Published by Arco Publishing Company, Inc.
219 Park Avenue South, New York, N.Y. 10003

Library of Congress Cataloging in Publication Data

Stecken, Fritz.
   Training the horse and rider.

   1. Dressage.
I. Title

SF309.5.S73   798'.23   72-2706
ISBN 0-668-03786-5

Printed in the United States of America

To my daughters
Carolyn and Rosalie
and
to the talented and interested riders of the
United States of America

Acknowledgments

I must extend my thanks to Mr. and Mrs. Donald A. Lester of Thornton, Pennsylvania, for their hospitality to me while I was writing this book.

I must also mention Mr. August Staeck and Mr. Otto Loerke in order to pay respect and to honor both gentlemen for their contributions to authentic dressage as it is known and universally accepted today.

And my very great thanks to my typists, Teresa Voellmecke and Adelle Gaillard.

Contents

Training the Horse and Rider

Foreword

My acquaintance with Fritz Stecken goes back many years—to when I was assigned as Instructor and Olympic Jumping Team Member from Hungary to the Krampnitz Cavalry in Germany in order to study and evaluate their method of training.

This book is the unique product of a man of tremendous experience in the field of riding.

It is not necessary to agree with all the details and explanations on the subject of training a dressage and rider, but one thing is certain—Fritz Stecken produced horses for the highest level performances in the shortest time and he was able to explain what he was doing. There were and are not too many gifted with this talent.

I am convinced that the study of this book will help many seriously interested riders to successfully practice the true art of riding.

Bertalan de Nemethy

Introduction

Shortly before the death of General Guy V. Henry, Chairman of the U.S. Equestrian Advisory Committee, I had a conversation with him about the United States' standing in International competition. He expressed his wish that I write a book expanding the guidelines that the Advisory Committee had published under his Chairmanship. It was his hope that such a book would help future generations to learn the scientific and classical art of riding, since it was apparent that an enormous interest in dressage was developing. It was a great privilege and honor for me to be asked by General Henry to help him in his efforts to improve the standard of riding for International and Olympic competition. Because of my high esteem for General Henry, I gladly complied with his wish, and as a result have written this book in his memory.

In the early days of dressage in the United States, the outlook was not very promising. Only one book was available on the subject in the English language. Other translated books which followed confused many riders, instructors, and judges. Our first selected dressage riders (officers as well as civilians) had a disadvantage in competition against riders from other countries since they could not gain experience at shows while performing in front of spectators, judges, and other riders. The enormous upswing in interest in dressage now offers all riders the chance to compete year round in all tests; this is mostly due to the efforts of the Pony Clubs and dressage organizations.

It is my hope and intention in writing this book to clarify some of the mystery surrounding the word "dressage." Translated from the French, which was the official language of the Fédération Equestre Internationale (F.E.I.) in the founding years, the word simply means "training." The objective of dressage is to train the horse and the rider and lead both to one unity, or harmony, whether for jumping, eventing, or riding intricate figures.

After the 1972 Olympic Games, one could read the following statement about our dressage team in a European magazine: "The American riders must understand that dressage is not circling around in the ring by riding figures. Dressage is suppleness and flexibility to the highest degree possible."

Major St. Cyr of Sweden, the Olympic Gold Medalist of 1952 and 1956, said in a speech made in Germany: "Dressage must be the result of systematic and gymnastic training. The assumption that there is a Germanic or Romanic method is wrong."

We still have the mistaken assumption that dressage is some sort of exhibition. It is very easy to gain approval from the public when exhibiting, but gaining success and approval in the eyes of experts from different countries is very difficult. It is of vital importance that the rider trains his horse to express itself in lightness, harmony, and beauty while accurately executing every gait, pace, and figure of the tests.

It is important to remember that the rules of the F.E.I. were formulated to make it possible for all member nations and all riders to accomplish for themselves the universally accepted standard set out by the F.E.I. These rules were developed by evaluation of the combined knowledge of all riding masters of the past as well as of the regulations each nation had for its own cavalry (see Appendixes II and III).

Article 401, The Object and General Principles of the F.E.I., reads as follows:

1. The object of Dressage is the harmonious development of the physique and ability of the horse. As a result, it makes the horse calm, supple, and keen, thus achieving perfect understanding with its rider.

2. These qualities are revealed by:
   a. the freedom and regularity of the paces;
   b. the harmony, lightness, and ease of the movements;
   c. the lightness of the forehand and the engagement of the hindquarters;
   d. the horse remaining absolutely straight in any movement along a straight line and bending accordingly when moving on curved lines.

3. The horse thus gives the impression of doing of his own accord what is required of him. Confident and attentive, he submits generously to the control of his rider.

4. His walk is regular, free, and unconstrained. His trot is free, supple, regular, sustained, and active. His canter is united, light, and cadenced. His quarters are never inactive or sluggish. They respond to the slightest indication of the rider and thereby give life and spirit to all the rest of his body.

5. By virtue of a lively impulsion and the suppleness of his joints, free from the paralyzing effects of resistance, the horse obeys willingly and without hesitation and responds to the various aids calmly and with precision.

Dr. Rainer Klimke on *Mehmed* (West Germany).

6. In all his work, even at the halt, the horse must be on the bit. A horse is said to be "on the bit" when the hocks are correctly placed, the neck more or less raised according to the extension or collection of the pace, the head remains steadily in position, the contact with the mouth is light, and no resistance is offered to the rider.
7. The position of the horse when "on the bit" depends on the conformation as well as on the degree of training of the horse.

The requirements for a dressage horse competing under F.E.I. rules are that *the horse must be relaxed and balanced, and must perform accurately and with the utmost forward impulsion.* Riders with the ambition to train themselves beyond the requirements of the Pony Clubs must start, from the beginning, by observing the fundamental requirements of the F.E.I. The proper training is evidenced by a horse which performs in a relaxed manner; executes the tests harmoniously and with balance; shows self-carriage during the execution of the tests; and performs accurately with the utmost forward impulsion and with lateral and longitudinal flexibility. To achieve these fundamental requirements, the U.S. Equestrian Advisory Committee, under General Henry's chairmanship, published the A, B, and C level tests in the pamphlet *Notes on Dressage.* These tests are reprinted in this book.

In this book I have tried to make clear, in a simple way, the methods a rider can use to accomplish the correct training of his horse so that he can compete in conformance with the F.E.I. requirements. Since horses and riders differ in their sensitivity and responses, it is a great help to the rider to have proper guidelines. The rider should train his horse within the framework of these guidelines, while the judge should observe whether or not the horse and rider fulfill the requirements. The methods presented here were written so that the horse could be trained under the most basic rule; *to force or discipline a horse is unnecessary, irrelevant, and absolutely wrong.*

Every rider, male or female, can train a horse to the highest level when he or she can guide the horse through all the exercises through the legs from behind to the front. At this point, training the horse is a technique to coordinate the rider's aids. The more this technique is refined the better the horse's performance will be. Mediocre performances are always the result of drilling or forcing a horse—not the result of gymnastic training to develop the natural ability of the horse, which is the true meaning of dressage or the classical art of riding. This can be done only individually, because of the differences in sensitivity in horses and riders. A nervous rider will not get along with a sensitive horse, and a cold-blooded horse will not do well with a phlegmatic rider. Both horse and rider should be evenly tempered. A few riders can train any horse, but they are an exception. The assumption that women cannot train a horse is, I believe, very foolish and presumptuous. Women are often more suited for Thoroughbred and Saddlebred horses than male riders are, since their gentle and sensitive handling is better adapted to these high-strung horses. I have seen many such horses spoiled by the rough and aggressive training habits of some male riders.

Riders who wish to enter competition will be able to find many good and suitable horses. Horses whose hocks are too far apart, horses with sway backs, horses with too-narrow cheek bones, and horses with temperamental difficulties should not be chosen to be trained to a high level. These horses have physical difficulties which will cause them to resist and refuse the highest degree of collection. It is waste of time and effort to try to train one of them above the Pony Club level; but many suitable and beautiful horses are available for higher training.

Mrs. Karen Schlueter on *Liostro* (West Germany).
(Photograph by Karl Schonersted.)

A horse's expression is his way of moving while executing the tests, and his appearance should be decisive in choosing him as a candidate for competition in the Grand Prix de Dressage at the International and Olympic level, since it will have a bearing on his score in the test.

It is my conviction that many talented young people and other interested riders, given their ability and desire to ride well and the availability of suitable horses, can greatly improve their riding and training methods by following the guidelines expressed in this book. By practicing the prescribed exercises and figures, the rider will discover that his horse will become much more sensitive and responsive to his aids. Further, by using his aids properly, the rider will be able to achieve the desired results in all gaits, paces, and figures on single- and two-tracks. The rider should remember that leg-yielding is a suppling exercise, while shoulder-in is a collecting exercise; no rider should over- or under-estimate one or the other. It is also important to remember that the training of the horse and rider must be done systematically and methodically, with patience and diligence, on a daily basis; and that the horse must remain relaxed and balanced at all times, which means that the rider must also be relaxed. Every rider can rest assured that daily riding will make his muscles stronger, and that his ability to influence his horse with a stronger driving seat will therefore improve. The coordination of his aids will consequently refine his riding technique. The rider will then be able to adapt himself individually to each horse he trains—whether it is for jumping, eventing, or riding classical dressage tests.

Hopefully, our National Dressage Federation will issue guidelines under which instructors can guide their students and judges can judge uniformly, so that U.S. dressage riders will be able to find their own identity—as the three day event and jumping riders have—

with which to represent the U.S. in International and Olympic competition.

Regrettably, few other successful dressage riders have written books. They understood the time required and difficulty involved in writing down their thoughts and feelings about dressage as it is practiced in our time. They also realized, as I do, that training a horse is dependent upon the ability of the rider and his belief in the ability of his horse to be sensitive and responsive in executing the various exercises and figures required.

Many riders have trained, and still do train, horses in their own unique way to prepare them to achieve the highest standards in the development of the horse's natural abilities. This is the true meaning of dressage, and is manifested in the rules and regulations of the F.E.I. I am convinced that some of our riders of the older generation, and especially the creative and motivated young riders of the Pony Clubs, not only *can* but *will* become exponents of the classical art of riding.

Miss Ulla Hakamson on *Ajax* (Sweden). *(Photograph by Werner Menzendorf.)*

Chapter I

Basic Principles of Training

Every rider who has ever mounted a "green" horse knows that horses are timid by nature. For this reason, the rider should give his horse a firm foundation to which he can return at any time. Without training, the horse's body is not flexible. Also, a horse which is young or incorrectly trained will not understand the rider's aids. This must always be taken into consideration by the instructor and/or rider.

As the U. S. Equestrian Advisory Committee stated in *Notes on Dressage*, published in 1952:

> The training of a horse should progress in a systematic manner. He should not be asked to do difficult movements until his prior training has prepared him for the same. This applies to the rider as well.

The training of the horse starts with stabilizing the horse in the working gaits. Through his intuitive guidance, the rider is able to make the horse sensitive and responsive to his aids. Every horse will then move confidently, with regular and relaxed steps, in the walk, trot, and canter. Because of the horse's willingness to move forward from behind to the front, the rider is able to acquire a light and steady contact with the reins between his hands and the horse's mount—keeping the horse on the bit.

As General Henry stated in *Notes on Dressage*:

> A general line along which progressive training could proceed is shown by movements in the tests A-1 to C-1.

To give variety, three tests have been given for each category. (See Appendix V.) The tests themselves have been prepared for contest purposes. It is *not* intended that these prescribed tests should be used in daily training, but such training may well be held to the movements prescribed in each category of the tests as indicated:

Tests A-1, A-2, A-3: For horses and/or riders in their early training.

Tests B-1, B-2, B-3: For those in middle training.

Tests C-1, C-2, C-3: For those horses in advanced training, ridden by skillful riders with equestrian tact.

In the ordinary walk, trot, and canter, a horse should move freely forward in a natural way. In the strong gaits, the horse has to lengthen his base of support without going faster, but in longer steps and strides instead. Therefore, the silhouette of the horse varies in the three gaits. In the collected gaits, the horse appears more compressed, and in the extended gaits more expanded. The rider has to influence his horse with stronger driving aids to execute these gaits, since the collected and extended gaits must be executed in cadence. As stated in *Notes on Dressage:*

Mr. Josef Neckermann on *Mariano* (West Germany).

A well-schooled horse must travel straight, the hind legs following the front legs accurately. He must be flexible on both sides, must be light on the rider's aids, and must obey the aids promptly. He must go willingly and be comfortable under the rider, and must be steady on the bit. The head and neck must be steady and erect on the wither and shoulder without moving about. It should not be carried too low or too high, nor should it be carried too short or too long, regardless of conformation. The poll should always be the highest point of the horse. The horse should never toss its head, should never go behind the bit, and should never have its head behind the perpendicular, and should *not tilt its head.* The horse should be constantly balanced between the rider's legs and hands, and should be on the bit, gently chewing the bit with a closed mouth, and a *light, flexible feel.* In all gaits the horse must show marked forward impulsion and vigor, but particularly in the collected gaits. . . . Horses competing in dressage classes should show suppleness, flexibility, and regularity at all gaits, smoothness and correctness in executing all figures, precise and prompt obedience to the rider's aids, and constant vigorous forward impulsion with *free self-carriage.* Regardless of the level in which the horse is shown, his performance must be the result of systematic and gymnastic training.

The development of the gaits, paces, and figures using tests A-1 to C-3 will guarantee progressive and correct training up to the universally accepted F.E.I. tests. In the first stage, the rider must perfect his horse through balance, relaxation, and regularity in the ordinary and strong gaits, paces, and figures which the horse can perform on a single track. In the second stage, the rider can then perfect his horse through relaxation, balance, and regularity in the collected and extended gaits and paces and in the figures the horse can perform on a single- and two-tracks. Through these exercises the suppleness, flexibility, and impulsion improves so that the horse is able to perform the

F.E.I. tests correctly. It is helpful for the horse and rider to do leg-yielding in the first stage and shoulder-in in the second stage to reach perfection for International competition.

While practicing for these tests, riders will experience gradual progress in the skill of both horse and rider. The rider will be progressively better able to guide and feel the responses of his horse. The horse will begin to relax and will become balanced as a result; this in turn will cause regularity of his gaits. This effect can be achieved by practice in the working gaits. The horse will be able to move regularly and briskly forward and will drop his head and neck forward and downward from his withers—regardless of his origin (American, Austrian, French, German, Russian, etc.) or his breeding (Arabian, Morgan, Palomino, Saddlebred, or Thoroughbred). If the rider then feels contact with his horse's mouth, he knows that he has established the first degree of collection: the horse is then "on the bit." The rider must remember that the whole muscular system of the horse stretches from behind to the front. Exercises in the ordinary and strong paces and gaits and practice of the required figures while the rider keeps his hands fixed or relaxed will bring the horse to a higher degree of collection because of the continuous and increased bending of the joints of the hind legs due to strong forward impulsion. The horse will also increase the arch in his neck. A horse must relax all of his muscles to be light on the rider's hands.

Training the horse within the framework of the A, B, and C tests enables the rider to shorten or lengthen the horse's base of support. A horse of great jumping ability can be easily improved as a jumper up to International standards, as was *Democrat*, the outstanding jumper of the Fort Riley Cavalry School. A horse with a great ability to jump combined with boldness and stamina can become a strong contender as a three-day-

Mr. Ivan Kalita on *Tarif* (USSR). *(Photograph by Werner Menzendorf.)*

event horse of International standard, as was *Jenny Camp*, the outstanding three-day-event horse of the 1936 Olympics. Training for a higher standard in three-day-eventing has to be achieved by training the horse to meet some of the requirements of the C level tests. The training for shoulder-fore and shoulder-in is especially helpful for every three-day-event horse.

The proper fundamental training which a horse must have for stiff International dressage tests can be done without undue pressure on horse and rider in one year for each test category—A, B, C, and D. The training of a Grand Prix dressage horse must proceed meticulously from the A-1 test to the D-3 test. A horse with a naturally flexible body can reach the highest level in three years of training. Only the C level tests will give a horse the necessary foundation for the F.E.I. tests.

Even a finish-trained Grand Prix dressage horse needs to be limbered up in the working gaits. In these gaits, a properly trained horse can use his muscles in a relaxed manner. A Grand Prix dressage horse should have well-developed muscles but the rider should not ask the horse to use his muscles fully all of the time. This fact is often overlooked by riders. A rider should never overwork his horse by riding figures for the sake of riding figures. The horse's muscles must be developed, since the suppleness of the muscles makes it possible for the horse to bend his joints. Every horse can walk, trot, and canter, but the horse must also carry the rider's weight, and it is not accustomed to this in the beginning. This extra weight causes the horse to tighten its back muscles, and these muscles move the limbs of the horse. The rider must therefore accustom the horse to carrying his weight and so the horse can relax its muscles. Only a relaxed muscle can be strengthened. This is important for the rider as well. A stiff and rigid seat will result if the rider cannot relax his own muscles.

Every judge, instructor, and rider must be aware of the horse's relaxation, balance, suppleness, and flexibility. The rider must also know which exercises will improve his horse's training gradually and progressively.

The key word is *relaxation,* "to attain an equilibrium state." From this a horse will, if the rider does not interfere with his hands, find his *balance,* "the stability produced by an even distribution of weight on each side of the vertical axis."

A horse which has been trained so that the rider can influence it with his legs will step forward with its hind legs to reach the hoofprints of the forehand. This must be clearly visible in the working, ordinary, and especially the collected gaits. It is proof of the ability of the horse to bend its hip joints. Only in this way is the weight of the horse and rider evenly distributed, and the horse able to move in self-carriage. Self-carriage can be readily observed in horses moving in freedom in the pasture.

When the rider has trained his horse so that it can execute all gaits while remaining relaxed and balanced, he can start with increasing and decreasing the gaits and paces and introduce his horse to the fundamental figures. The rider should use these exercises repeatedly to develop the strength of the muscles.

The horse's body must reach the highest degree of suppleness and flexibility through the use of appropriate exercises. Every muscle in the horse's body should be strengthened and every joint should be made flexible. When the rider trains his horse through the first stage in the training period, he provides a good foundation for either a hunter, jumper, three-day-event, or Grand Prix dressage horse. A Grand Prix dressage horse must also be trained through all of the exercises of the second stage.

The rider has to train his horse according to the

Mr. Kissimoff on *Ikhor* (USSR).

horse's natural way of moving in the walk, trot, and canter in order to obtain the horse's relaxation and balance. These gaits are known as the "working gaits." With this foundation, every rider can develop all gaits, paces, and figures which a horse can perform on a single track. Through riding transitions by increasing and decreasing all gaits, the horse's longitudinal flexibility will improve. Through these exercises, the rider can develop the ordinary gaits.

The most important factor in training a horse is the rider's seat. A good seat is needed to guide the horse through the necessary exercises as well as to jump or ride through the tests. The rider will become frustrated if the horse resists and is unresponsive to his aids, and, more important, the rider will be helpless in executing figures if the horse is not responsive.

The guidelines which instructors and riders have are of great importance. Within the framework of these guidelines, the rider can approach the training and teaching of this horse properly. The approach to training each horse must be different, since horses and riders differ in their feelings, sensitivity, and responsiveness; as far as horses are concerned, this is often misunderstood as intelligence.

All horses must be able to use their back muscles. Every horse will become obedient when he can use this muscle in a completely relaxed manner, and will lower his head and neck accordingly. The long muscle of the neck will become visible on both sides of the horse. This is proof that the horse is relaxed, and should be seen even in the highest degree of collection, such as the pirouette and the piaffe. Shortening of the horse's neck through the influence of the rider's hands is irrelevant to the horse's proper collection. Relaxation is also evidenced by the horse holding both ears slightly back—a sign that he is attentive to the rider. The ears should move forward only if the horse sees something which interests him or when the horse and rider approach a jump. Another sign of relaxation is when the horse carries his tail higher in the gaits.

Only when the back muscle is used in a relaxed way can the horse move his limbs freely and carry the rider forward with the proper impulsion. The stronger this back muscle becomes the more the horse is able to bend his joints, especially his hip joints which are vital in jumping, eventing, or performing dressage tests.

The horse must be trained to become supple and flexible. Under the most favorable conditions, the rider receives only 20 percent of the total score for performance. The horse receives the remainder for executing the gaits and figures in conformance with the rules of the F.E.I. The rider must accept the fact that he is not participating in a beauty or popularity contest. It is not important that the rider can ride the Grand Prix test. What *is* important is the impression a horse executing the test is able to give to the judges.

To train a horse a horse the rider must first obtain the horse's confidence, and from this, the horse's relaxation. With these, the rider can develop the horse's regularity and flexibility in all gaits and paces. The rider is able, when riding transitions and exercises on single- and two-tracks, to get the flexibility necessary to ride his horse in collection, extension, and cadence. The rider can train the horse to accomplish this only with a correct seat. The correct seat enables the rider to give the aids a horse needs to perform all the necessary exercises. The horse has to be given these aids to be trained from the first stage to the last stage of training, as required by the F.E.I. The rider must take into consideration the fact that the horse's body is not flexible by nature, and that these qualities must be patiently acquired. The only communication a rider has with his horse is through his seat. The rider's legs, back, and hands have to be coordinated so that the rider can

Mr. Bruce Davidson on *Irish Cap* (USA). *(Photograph by Alix Coleman.)*

guide his horse through the necessary exercises under the influence of his seat.

It is of great importance for the rider to study the skeletal and muscular systems of the horse in order to know and be able to feel which muscles have to be strengthened and which joints of his horse have to be made more flexible. He must understand that suppleness refers to the muscular system, and flexibility to the skeletal system.

The most important muscle is the horse's back muscle. The action of this muscle sets the limbs in motion, and stronger activity of this muscle gives the horse regular steps and strides in cadence.

The most important joint is the horse's hip joint. This joint narrows and widens when the horse is in motion. The stifle moves up and down and, in all two-track movements, also moves sidewards. It not only makes it possible for the horse to thrust himself off the ground elastically, thus enabling him to push his body vigorously forward, but also enables the horse to lower his croup by flexing this joint further and carrying more of his weight on his hind legs. This action on the horse's part is what is meant by the expressions "engaging the hocks" and "engaging the hind legs."

Through riding transitions, increasing and decreasing the gaits and paces, and changing from one gait to another, the flexibility and suppleness of the horse increase progressively—as in the A, B, C, and D tests. Progressive training in these exercises will make the horse's body more flexible and supple. For a rider who wishes to train his horse for jumping or eventing only, the A and B level exercises should provide a good foundation.

The rider should ask his horse for the ordinary and strong paces in the A and B tests. In the C and D tests, a horse can and should be asked for the collected and extended paces. At this stage, every horse will move in cadence by lowering his croup and by bending the joints of his hind legs. The shoulder freedom must be clearly noticeable, and the motion of the front legs should become light and graceful. The rider will be able to feel the suppleness of the horse's spine by concentrating on feeling how he sits *in* and not *on* the horse, directly behind the horse's shoulder blades. The horse will arch his neck and erect his head by himself when given the appropriate exercises.

The third test in each training period gives the rider proof of how much his horse has been perfected during the period. The strong gaits—in other words, lengthening the base of support—are the foundation for executing the collected and extended gaits properly. It is of fundamental importance to have the horse correctly perform the C1, C2, and C3 tests. The D and F.E.I. tests can be ridden correctly only if a horse is made flexible both longitudinally and laterally. It is not difficult to train a horse to the highest standard. Once the horse's balance, responsiveness, and sensitivity are established, the rider will be surprised to learn how much *more* sensitive and responsive his horse can become. In fact, the rider will be able to ride all tests with completely invisible aids, and also by guiding the horse with the reins held in one hand.

The D tests were designed to be substituted for the F.E.I. tests in order to prevent the rider from drilling and mechanizing his horse. While riding tests, the horse should not learn to anticipate the figures. A horse has to be trained to move in regular and relaxed steps and strides going forward. The rhythm has to be the same in the ordinary or strong walk, trot, or canter. In the strong paces, the horse must gain more ground by lengthening his steps or strides; in other words, he must lengthen his base of support. This is of fundamental importance, since otherwise the horse cannot be correctly trained to perform the collected and ex-

Mr. Otto Loerke on *Fanal,* riding with reins in one hand. Note the complete relaxation, suppleness, and flexibility combined with utmost forward impulsion.

tended gaits and the figures required in International competition. Dressage tests specify certain gaits and figures which a horse has to perform, but these gaits and figures are only means to an end, and not the vital object of dressage. The F.E.I. states this in the rules for dressage events in article 401. (Articles 100 and 101 state the purpose behind the rules and regulations.) *

Horses must first be trained to perform ordinary and strong gaits and in figures which a horse can perform with regular steps and strides on a single-track with strong forward impulsion. It is also a fact that a horse first responds only to one-sided aids. These are the outside leg and hand and, after the rider has accomplished this, the inside leg and hand. For this reason the horse and rider should first learn to perform leg-yielding and figures in which the rider can guide his horse with his legs and maintain brisk forward impulsion in the ordinary and strong gaits.

The rider should begin leg-yielding as soon as the horse has confidence in him and moves willingly forward while remaining relaxed and balanced in all three gaits. Leg-yielding enables the horse to move briskly forward on a single- or two-tracks through the influence of the rider's legs. It also limbers up the horse's spine, ribs, and hip and shoulder joints. These portions of the horse's body cannot be exercised with the rider's hands, but only through the influence of his legs. This fundamental exercise will improve the horse's longitudinal and lateral flexibility to the utmost. Through leg-yielding, the rider can influence his horse with his legs so that the horse's hind hoofs step forward to reach the hoofprints of the front legs. This is important, since only then can the rider develop the power of the horse's hind legs to push forward in order

* See page 202.

to lighten the forehand in the collected gaits and go in cadence.

Most riders use their hands too much, impairing the horse's natural way of moving. This is the reason that the horse resists. Leg-yielding is the most important suppling exercise for the horse, up to and including the Grand Prix level, and will help to reduce resistance on the part of the horse. Only through leg-yielding can the rider make his horse sensitive and responsive to his legs so that he may ride his horse from behind to the front. The horse will be able to bend his joints and therefore be able to stay light on the bit by arching his neck. Riders who attempt to achieve this with their hands will only provoke resistance, and instead of keeping the horse relaxed and balanced, they will unintentionally strengthen the ability of the horse's muscles to resist, making the joints stiffer. Draw reins and chambons should be used only scarcely and only when absolutely necessary. Inexperienced riders should never be allowed to use them.

Leg-yielding is the first exercise on two-tracks and should therefore be done only at the walk. Leg-yielding teaches the rider to use his legs properly so that the horse will respond to them. In all two-track movements, the horse has to be bent by the rider's outside leg around his inside leg. The rider has to learn how to accomplish this, and the horse has to be trained to respond to the rider's leg by bending his body evenly from poll to tail.

It is very simple to develop the shoulder-in from leg-yielding with the inside leg. The U.S. Advisory Committee defined the shoulder-in as the inside hind leg following the outside front leg without crossing at a 30 to 35 degree angle. In leg-yielding the horse's legs *do* cross and the angle is about 45 degrees. Shoulder-in performed as defined by the Advisory Committee helps the horse and rider to maintain impulsion and cadence. However, it can be performed only after the horse can bend his ribs and spine laterally and will accept the rider's legs to move sidewards. Leg-yielding provides the foundation. The definition of shoulder-in as written in the F.E.I. book was never debated because the shoulder-in is not required by the F.E.I. tests. The German L.P.O. (Leistungs-prufung-ordnung) guidelines, which are decisive in preparing German civilian riders for International competition, state the definition as follows: "In shoulder-in the horse moves in the opposite direction from which it is bent. The hind legs go on the track and the front legs are at least a half step from the track of the outside front leg."

The correct shoulder-in is the key to all collected and extended gaits and figures. Through it, the rider is able to influence his horse to maintain the impulsion and cadence, thus lowering the croup and lightening the front legs. The perfection of the shoulder-in is also crucial for all requirements of the F.E.I. tests. Only riders who are able to get this perfection from their horses will be successful in International competition. It is the key in developing the natural ability of a horse to the highest degree of perfection in longitudinal and lateral flexibility.

A rider who wants to represent his country and compete against selected horses and riders from other countries must start with himself, and must prepare himself mentally and physically. He then has to find and train a horse which has natural balance, gaits, and looks. The rider has to realize that he is only as good as his horse, notwithstanding the amount that he glorifies himself in writing, in entertaining, or in criticizing. The more that nature gave to the horse in the way of balance, looks, and style of moving, the greater the chance the rider will have in his training and in competition. This type of horse is not difficult to find.

Mr. August Staeck on *Hammer* and Mr. Fritz Stecken on *Waldkater* in Aachen, West Germany, 1938.

Every interested rider has to bear in mind that dressage means training, not exhibiting. Horse and rider must have a good foundation. The rider must sit correctly so that he is not interfering with the horse's balance. The horse must move forward naturally and briskly, remaining balanced and relaxed, in the walk, trot, and canter. With such a foundation, many horses and riders can reach the highest degree of horsemanship.

Riders who want to compete in the Grand Prix de Dressage in International events have to bear in mind that they must ride the test individually, and not in uniformity as done by a group of soldiers in a drill. The rules and regulations of the F.E.I. and the guidelines of the Fédération Nationale (F.N.) are not orders which the rider must obey. They are simply helpful suggestions, and the rider is free to train his horse according to his own feeling. The rider must individualize himself to each horse he trains.

The rider should train his horse scientifically, methodically, and systematically before riding the F.E.I. tests. This must be done so that the horse can use his body correctly. In International and Olympic competition the rider should have his horse trained so that it is possible for the horse to express himself through performing the required gaits, paces, and figures. The impression the horse gives to the judge decides the score for the whole performance of the test. The rider has to be creative before his riding can be called a classical art. It is erroneous to think about classical performing or baroque movements. Every movement is classical when the rider has developed the horse's natural way of moving through the appropriate exercises. The A, B, and C tests published in this book give a progressive program with which to train the horse step-by-step up to the F.E.I. level. These tests were designed for all horses—not for any one rider.

Chapter II

The Logical and Progressive
Training of Horse and Rider

Riding is feeling—a rapport which prompts the rider to give his horse the proper aids. Dressage is a physical training course for the horse, and is known as the classical art of riding. This training does not concern itself with producing a flashy looking horse, but rather a horse which is well-balanced, supple, obedient to the rider, and comfortable to ride.

This book has been written to help young people and other interested riders understand more clearly the meaning of the word "dressage," and to remove the mystery surrounding the word. Dressage is the methodical and systematic training of the horse and rider, and it is not as difficult as some riders might think. This is particularly true if the rider makes certain that the horse remains relaxed and balanced during the first stages of training and throughout the training period. This point cannot be stressed too strongly. Also, frequent riding without stirrups helps the rider to feel the proper coordination of the aids and strengthens his muscles—all very important in the training of the horse.

At the present time, a misconception exists regarding the correct procedure for the teaching and training of the horse. This misconception is the reason for so much confusion and disagreement among nations and their riders. It leads to drilling—as opposed to training—the horse, and consequently to resistance by the horse and punishment by the rider. *The proper (or gymnastic) training of a horse enables him to perform with complete relaxation, suppleness, and flexibility.*

It must be stressed that through every hour of the horse's training, whether beginning or advanced, the most important fundamentals are regularity of gait, vigorous forward impulsion, evenness of the horse's body to both sides, and a light and steady contact with the bit. If these requirements are not met perfectly, the horse's training is *incorrect,* no matter how many fancy gaits and figures he can perform.

The greatest mistake a rider can make is to succumb to the urge to show off his horse in some spectacular or unusual way. He must consistently bear in mind the fact that his sole aim must be simply to develop whatever natural abilities his horse's individual conformation permits.

The basic purpose of dressage is to produce the kind of horse and rider universally accepted as beautiful to see: exhibiting grace, balance, lightness, ease, fluidity of movement, and enthusiasm for work (which may be expressed as forward impulsion). The horse exhibits these qualities naturally in freedom, but it takes special training to make him appear with the same beauty while under a rider. Development of the horse's body through dressage should allow the horse to move with all of his natural freedom and grace under the rider—whether on the flat, over jumps, or cross-country.

This method of training is a series of exercises designed to strengthen every muscle and supple every joint in the horse's body. When a horse has been worked daily for several months, a marked improvement will be noted in his gaits, ease of turning, and sensitivity to the rider.

Much of the work, particularly in the early stages, should be done on the longe line. It is important that the trainer stand in one spot, so that the horse makes a perfect circle around him. If side reins are used they must be adjusted to the length of the horse's neck: not too long, since the horse must feel the bit; and not too short, since the horse must not be restricted in his movements. As the horse moves in a perfect circle on both hands, he will flex his body slightly toward the direction in which he is going. The trainer (and rider) must see that the horse's spine is bent evenly from poll to tail, so that his front and hind prints are in the same track, and so that he does not carry his hindquarters in or out. The horse must move forward briskly and with even steps, bringing his hind feet well under his body. He must move forward freely into the bit, mouthing it gently, but with no attempt to use it for support.

When mounted exercises are commenced, the horse must move forward in the same brisk, even manner, traveling perfectly straight when required, and bending accurately and smoothly in turns. His first mounted lessons (other than going straight ahead in a steady, relaxed, but energetic manner) will be in large circles, with the same bending practice as on the longe line. Next, he may be worked in serpentines of large, but always even, loops.

Gradually, a few steps at a time, he may be introduced to exercises on two-tracks; that is, where the hind prints do not follow the front prints. In two-track exercises the horse becomes more sensitive to the rider's legs, and since a constant slight bending of the body is required in all two-track movements, the horse

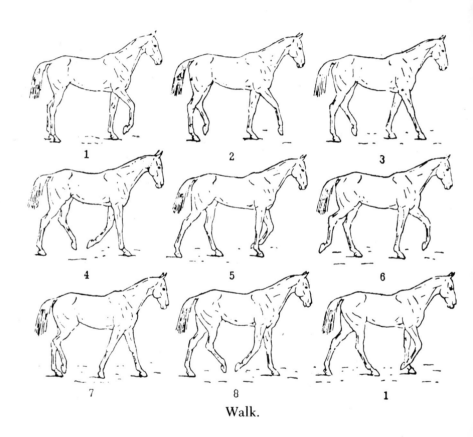

Walk.

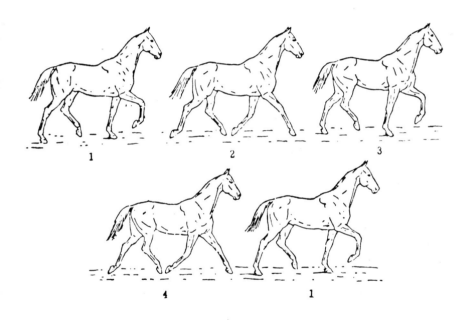

Trot.

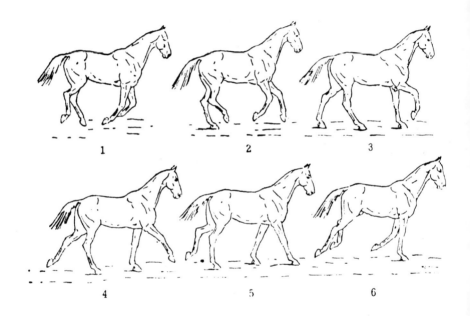

Canter.

becomes more supple laterally.

Throughout this work the rider must always watch for regularity of gait, vigorous forward impulsion, evenness in the bend of the horse's body to both sides, and a steady contact with the bit. This is possible only in ordinary and strong gaits, because no cadence is required and the rider can develop the power of the horse's hind legs to push his and the rider's body forward. The rider must subordinate his eagerness to produce certain advanced movements and figures to a desire for absolute perfection in the horse's way of going, or he will defeat his own purpose.

A horse with about as much training as we have described will make a delightful pleasure horse. Along with the exercises mentioned, he must be given long, free rides on the bridlepath, path, work over cavalletti, and practice over low jumps.

If the trainer desires to further develop the horse's flexibility and suppleness, and if he shows a talent for this work, more collected training may be commenced. Collected and extended gaits develop the power of the horse's hind legs to carry his own weight and that of his rider. He is worked in the canter at the counterlead; from this he can be trained to execute a correct flying change. More difficult two-tracking movements can be practiced, such as two-tracking on the diagonal at the walk, trot, and canter, with flying changes on changing direction. As his balance and sensitivity improve, he will be able to make flying changes on a straight line, finally being able to change on every stride. At the canter, he will be able to execute the pirouette, which is a turn on the haunches while cantering without gaining ground. At the trot, the finest exhibitions of precision are the piaffe—trot in place; and the passage—a high, cadenced trot which gains ground slowly. He will be able to exhibit balance and suppleness, both longitudinally and laterally.

Counterlead.

Pirouette (left).

Piaffe.

Although some countries have had classes for dressage horses for many years, dressage is still in the beginning stage in the United States. Interest in this method of training is growing, especially thanks to the extensive influence of the United States Pony Club. The general usefulness of dressage is becoming more widely appreciated.

Because dressage classes require that the horse perform specified gaits and figures, these gaits and figures are often misconstrued as the vital object of dressage. However, they are only a means to an end; merely a vehicle for exhibiting the degree of suppleness and poise the horse possesses at different stages of his training.

After stabilizing the horse in the working gaits, the rider must first perfect the ordinary gaits: a free, swinging, ordinary, and strong walk; an enthusiastic ordinary and strong trot of metronome precision; a springy ordinary and strong canter that threatens neither to get out of control nor to become sluggish. At all gaits the horse must constantly remain on the rider's aids. The first prerequisite for this is that the horse be relaxed and in balance: his hip joints flexing freely to allow his hind legs to step well under the body. The horse can then carry himself in "good posture" without leaning on the bit. He will be sensitive and immediately responsive to the rider's aids, being propelled forward step-by-step and stride-by-stride by the swinging action of his back. The horse's spine will be kept in a straight line from poll to tail by the rider's legs, which must always be in contact with the horse's sides. A light, steady contact will be felt between the rider's hands and the horse's mouth.

In all stages of his training, the horse's carriage is of fundamental consideration. *If he does not carry himself properly, his basic training has been wrong.* His hip joints must be supple, his hindquarters well under, his back muscles relaxed, his forehand light, his neck

Passage.

Ordinary Trot (Saddlebred).

stretched long and more or less arched according to the degree of collection asked. His body must be perfectly straight in straight movements without carrying his hindquarters to one side or the other; his head must not be tilted sideward with one ear lower than the other. His steps must be free, vigorous, and regular in ordinary and strong gaits. Collected and extended gaits should be in cadence.

The rider should practice on large circles, 60 to 70 feet in diameter, first at a brisk sitting trot (in both directions) until the horse can stay effortlessly in a perfect circle, his body bent continuously in an even, gentle arc. These lessons must never be kept up until they become tedious for the horse, but must be alternated with long, relaxing rides straight ahead. Preferably, much of this riding should be done on bridlepaths.

The rider must bear in mind that the purpose of the circling exercises is to gently supple the horse laterally to both sides. His neck, ribs, and entire spine must continuously be evenly bent or the work will be of no real value.

When the horse is supple enough to trot easily, smoothly, and vigorously in a large circle, he may be allowed to break into a canter from the trot, gradually working up to the same smooth, calm, but energetic performance in the canter on both hands. Later the canter is commenced from a walk, rather than the trot. This improves the horse's longitudinal flexibility.

One of the best exercises for developing the horse's longitudinal flexibility is the cavalletti—an arrangement of poles laid parallel on the ground and spaced so that the horse can be trotted over them, stepping between the poles. Three or more poles should be spaced at distances of about three and one-half to five feet, according to the natural step of the horse. The cavalletti is also excellent preparation for a calm and balanced approach to jumping. Low jumps and long, free, cross-

Strong Trot (Thoroughbred).

Ordinary Canter (Palomino).

country rides are important at the early stage of training to increase the horse's longitudinal flexibility—suppling his hip joints and back—so that the more collected work will be easier for him.

The basic maxim for the dressage rider to bear in mind is *"Keep your horse straight and ride him forward"*—Gustav Steinbrecht. "Keep your horse straight" means that he must be laterally supple—able to bend evenly to both sides in curved figures or turns. "Ride him forward" refers to the horse's longitudinal suppleness—the free, swinging gaits which are only possible as a result of litheness and flexibility in the hindquarters. It might also be said, "keep him relaxed," for when horse or rider becomes tense all suppleness is lost and any work done is against the purpose of developing the natural freedom and grace.

The A tests used in this book are the easiest, progressing 1, 2, 3, then the B, C, and D tests. The three day event dressage test can be executed by a horse trained up to the C tests.

The tests reflect the general stages in the horse's regular training routine. In his daily work, the rider must not drill the horse in the sequence of figures of the test, but should practice the requirements of each test separately and gradually until they are perfected according to the horse's individual abilities.

Riders who want to achieve training by discipline or force are doomed to failure. Unintentionally, the rider strengthens the muscles of the horse to resist and the joints become stiffer. As a result, the horse either breaks down or resists so violently that the rider can be injured. On the other hand, the knowledgeable rider *can* ensure that the training is enjoyable for the horse and for himself.

Most riders have to work by themselves. The rider should first learn how to longe the horse. This will cause the horse to relax, and the relaxation will come as

Strong Canter (Thoroughbred).

soon as the horse has confidence in his trainer. These two factors are of the greatest importance. Only at this point can *any* rider begin to use his driving aids so that the horse finds his balance and regularity. As soon as the horse goes willingly and relaxed on the longe line, he can be allowed to go alone (free longed) in a small enclosure of 50 by 50 or 60 by 60 feet, with a fence of the height one sees around pastures.

If side reins are not used when longeing, the rider should make a knot at the end of the reins and put them behind the stirrups. When he feels the pressure on the bit, every horse will learn to give to the bit and the rider will be able to observe his horse's way of moving. The reins must never be made short. The horse must be able to walk, trot, and canter freely. In this way, all horses quickly learn to respond to the rider's hands.

Under a rider, or on the longe line, a horse will use his back muscles to move his hind legs and will then be able to bend his hip joints. The horse can be urged to step in the footprints of his front feet with his hind legs in the walk and trot. In the canter, the horse can use his hind legs, bringing them freely forward. In this way every horse will move in a relaxed and balanced manner in the three gaits.

As a result of the relaxation, every horse will slow down and will stretch his head and neck forward and downward. The rider must then use both legs to urge the hind legs to step forward to the bit so that the rider is able to keep a light and steady contact between his hands and the horse's mouth. This is the lowest degree of collection. Riders who learn to ride partially without supervision are usually able to get this first degree of collection on their own.

Riders not far enough advanced, and therefore not steady enough with their hands, should use side reins. These must be long so that the horse has freedom to

Working trot on the longeline without side reins.

Working trot under the rider (Thoroughbred).

stretch his neck. No rider should use sliding reins or chambons: they restrict the use of the muscles of the horse and therefore hinder the free forward movement. A horse must learn to carry himself by moving forward in a relaxed manner in the three gaits. The horse must find his head and neck carriage by himself, especially if the rider later wants to develop a Grand Prix Dressage horse. A "normal" head and neck carriage does not exist; it depends on the horse's conformation. The horse should bring his neck up from the withers so that the manecomb forms a slight arch from wither to poll. The poll should be the highest point, and the horse should hold his head so that his nose is slightly ahead of the vertical. The nose should be approximately on a level with the hip point. These are very important factors in training a horse up to the Grand Prix level.

Because it is important to the rider that his horse learn to use and bend the hip joints, this should be done when the horse is relaxed by riding outdoors as soon as possible. Also, by going uphill and downhill during long relaxing rides outdoors, the rider can establish the regularity of the gaits. Riders with "green" horses should ask riders with trained or quiet horses to accompany them on these rides outdoors. Almost all green horses will follow a quiet horse willingly. A complete relaxation of the entire muscular system will guarantee the rider's achieving a regular four-beat walk, a two-beat trot, and a three-beat canter. The rider must pay attention to his hands; they must never work backward, and the rider should not try to hold the horse's nose back and shorten the horse's neck. The horse should give the rider a light and steady contact between hands and mouth through the horse's forward impulsion. The length of each step and stride must be according to the individual horse's nature.

The rider can and must feel that his horse moves confidently, regularly, and briskly forward in the three

Working Walk.

Working Canter.

gaits. The rider can then feel through his seat how the horse's hindquarters and the forehand can be controlled with his aids. Only then should the rider start with the lateral training of his horse. The rider should stay within the framework of the requirements of the given test according to the strength of the horse's muscles and the flexibility of his joints.

A horse has to shorten or lengthen his base of support to stay balanced when going cross-country or over jumps. Therefore, a horse should be able to lengthen or shorten his steps or strides. At this point in his training, the horse's development will be furthered by riding many transitions in the three gaits. The ordinary and strong paces are the most comfortable paces for horse and rider. Through these paces, a horse is able to lengthen his steps and strides without going faster. He can stay balanced by covering more ground without losing the rhythm. In the beginning, no rider can avoid making the contact between his hands and the horse's mouth stronger while increasing the pace. By frequently giving half-halts and decreasing the paces, every horse can be trained to stay relaxed and balanced.

Riders who pay attention to their seat can feel that as soon as the horse accepts the half-halt he will erect himself. The horse will give this head and neck carriage to the rider by himself. The rider should never try to form the horse's neck carriage with his hands, as this only disturbs the horse's sequence in the gaits and restricts his free forward movement. This is the cause of the horse's disobedience and resistance. The training of the horse does not mean that the rider should compete with the horse's strength, but rather that the horse will use his power willingly and rationally with the rider whether going cross-country, over jumps, or executing intricate figures.

Many of our good and successful jumpers train their horses according to the ability of their horses. Training

Working Trot (Thoroughbred).

Working Trot (Saddlebred). All photographs of the working gaits show the natural way of moving without interference from the rider's hands.

a horse up to the International or Olympic level has to be done most thoroughly. It becomes more educational and refined in the three equestrian events under F.E.I. requirements. Instructors can be very helpful in suggesting that their students take into consideration the horse's psychological and physiological ability. It is wrong to assume that the horse learns psychologically by going from elementary to high school. He only learns to accept the aids which the rider uses to guide him through exercises which are necessary to improve him physically. The rider will then improve the horse's longitudinal and lateral flexibility naturally.

The training of the horse is becoming a creative art. The requirements of the Pony Clubs give instructors and riders ample opportunity to perfect this training on the fundamental level necessary for every horse and every rider. Horses which have difficulties in the working gaits and cannot be brought to a point where they can use their bodies properly can be helped by longeing and also by letting them step over cavalletti and low jumps. (See Chapter VI.)

This work can be done with or without the rider. Done patiently, it will bring every horse—green or incorrectly trained—to the point where he can relax and therefore be able to use his muscles and bend his joints. Every horse will gradually find his ordinary gaits from the working gaits by himself. To improve any horse, either for more advanced jumping or competition or for the dressage Grand Prix, the rider has to train his horse so that the longitudinal and lateral flexibility improves and the horse can use his hip joint like a spring. Green or older horses not accustomed to this work will show signs of fatigue, but after the prescribed exercises are wisely repeated, the horse will become well conditioned.

One very important point should be remembered by all riders: the rider should use his common sense and

Rodney Jenkins on *Idle Dice*, 1971. *(Photograph by Budd.)*

Michael Page on *Foster*, 1968. *(Photograph by Jean Bridel.)*

should not abuse the horse by kicking or hitting and jerking, especially a jerk which touches the most sensitive part of the horse—the mouth.

It is important that the rider study the skeletal and muscular systems of his horse. He should know exactly how the muscles and joints of the horse work. Most equine veterinarians will gladly help supply this knowledge. The rider needs to know this so that he can understand his horse and understand the necessity of performing the exercises described in the following chapters—exercises which are essential to further develop the horse's longitudinal and lateral flexibility.

Another point which must be stressed is that even if a rider wants to take a shortcut by buying a finished, trained horse he must first start with developing himself so that he can give the horse the proper aids. With a steady, light hand the rider can use his back effectively as a lever to influence the horse to move vigorously forward.

It is of great importance that the horse execute all figures in the relaxed and balanced manner which is a result of the suppling exercises. The rider can now train the horse in figures which require more longitudinal and lateral flexibility. After the horse has learned to yield to the rider's legs, it will require only a little practice to train him to execute the turn on the haunches. The best way to obtain this figure is to ride the horse first in a half-volt in the walk. Then, by giving half-halts, the rider can turn his horse in such a way that the horse's hind legs move in a smaller and smaller circle. The horse will respond by keeping his hind legs moving, which is very important. The horse is able, at this stage, to bend his hip joint, his spine, his ribs, and his neck. His body should be bent in the direction in which he is turning. After a relatively short time the horse will be able to turn on the haunches in place by pivoting around his inside hind leg. The

Kevin Freeman on *Good Mixture. (Photograph by Findlay Davidson.)*

horse must keep both hind legs moving and must not step backward. Backward movement is mostly the result of too strong an influence from the rider's hands. When the horse is able to turn correctly, the turn can be executed from the full stop. In the beginning, it is advisable to let the horse first take one step forward to avoid the inclination of most horses to step backward. If the rider's coordination between his legs, back, and hands is correct he will be able to ask the horse to turn with perfection—that is, the horse will set his inside hind leg in the same place from which it is lifted.

A very good exercise to improve the horse's flexibility is to lead the horse in a spiral-like turn. This should be done first in the walk, then in the trot, and later in the canter to the extent that the horse makes a small circle with his hind legs. The rider must use his outside leg strongly if necessary, and may have to bend his horse to the outside in order to make it possible for the horse to make such a small turn. Leg-yielding with the outside leg helps the rider to accomplish this in a relatively short period of time. To widen the small circle, the rider should lead the horse in a spiral-like turn back to the track of the circle with his inside leg. If necessary, the rider can use leg-yielding with the inside leg to get a response from the horse.

The rider who feels the horse stay willingly on the aids can now start to develop the counter-canter. After riding a half-volt in the corner following the long side of the working area, the rider should return to the track at an angle of 45 degrees. The rider must be certain that the horse maintains his balance by giving half-halts, especially while going through the corners. The rider must make the corners flat enough in the beginning so that the horse is able to keep his balance. It is advisable to ride a track big enough for a large circle. In this way the horse will be able to stay on the rider's aids, and in a short time he will establish his balance.

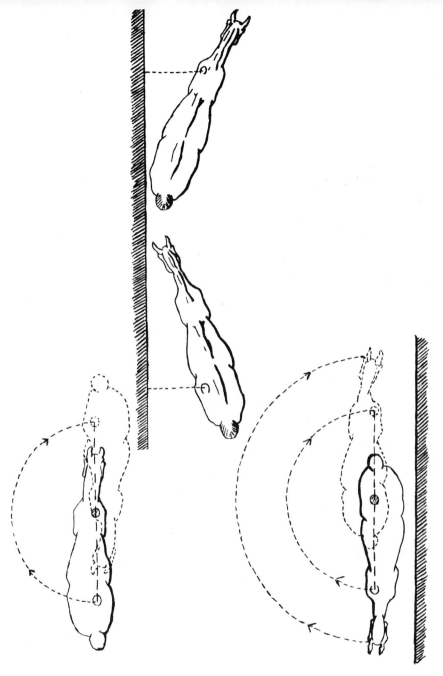

Turn on the fore and hind legs and leg-yielding with inside and outside leg.

Dave Kelly on *Sungirt*.

If the horse does not perform the figure correctly it is because he has difficulty remaining relaxed. The rider should not use force to accomplish this: patience and practice will ensure a good result. Bending the horse's neck to the outside temporarily will help the rider to achieve this. It is essential for the rider to keep the horse relaxed and balanced in the counter-canter. It is in this stage of the training that the rider feels the horse's spine and ribs bend to the inside and become supple. Now the rider is able to use diagonal aids— that is, his inside leg and outside rein. (The inside is always the side toward which the horse is bent, no matter in which direction the horse moves.)

It is now possible for the rider to influence the horse to move in the walk, trot, and canter with his shoulder-fore. The shoulder-fore is necessary for the horse to perform the tests up to the Grand Prix level gracefully and harmoniously in complete balance. To achieve the shoulder-fore movement the rider must bend the horse around his inside leg. It is possible for the horse to respond because he has learned from leg-yielding exercises to accept the rider's leg aid and bend his spine and ribs. The outside restraining rein pressing against the horse's neck will bring the horse's shoulder forward in such a way that the horse's inside hind leg steps between the horse's front legs. In this way the horse's inside hip joint and inside shoulder are in a straight line. This must be practiced in all gaits, ordinary and strong, as well as in the counter-canter or the strike-off to the canter. It is especially necessary in decreasing the paces as well as in changing gaits. The shoulder-fore must be practiced in both directions and with great patience and tact by the rider, since it is a time consuming effort for both horse and rider. By this time it should be possible for the rider to ride the horse correctly through tests B-1, B-2, and B-3.

If the horse cannot perform these tests in a relaxed

Mrs. Mary Chapot on *Tom Boy*. (*Photograph by Keith Money.*)

Miss Kathy Kusner on *King Night Hawk. (Foto Mitschke.)*

Mr. Frank Chapot, veteran member and now captain of the U.S. Prix of Nations jumping team, on *San Lucas.*
(Foto Mitschke.)

Championship Three Day Team at Burghley, England, 1974. They are (left to right): J. Michael Plumb on *Good Mixture*, Edward E. Emerson, Jr. on *Victor Dakin*, Donald W. Sachey on *Plain Sailing*, and Bruce Davidson on *Irish Cap*. (Photograph by Werner Ernst.)

and balanced manner with grace and impulsion, the rider must stabilize his horse with long and relaxing rides, possibly outdoors. Only then should the rider ask more from his horse. The rider can be assured that the further development of his horse's suppleness and flexibility will be more enjoyable for both horse and rider when done in this manner.

Riders are able to judge themselves if slow motion moving pictures are taken, and if they have enough self-criticism. This is inexpensive and easy to do, and very helpful. Taking such pictures from the front and from the side once or twice a year is very educational for the rider during the whole training program, especially for riders who have to ride mostly alone.

Riders who want to train their horses for hunting or jumping only will find that they must have control over their horses to increase, decrease, turn, and jump in a much easier way. Many horses can then be hunted and jumped on a snaffle bit.

Mr. de Nemethy and Mr. le Goff were very successful with their training method. Both recognized the basic purpose of dressage. All pictures of and the success by members of our three day and jumping teams clearly show why other nations and their media greatly admire and praise the perfect and successful style of our horses and riders in International and Olympic competition.

Equine and equestrian prospects abroad for all three equestrian Olympic events are prepared through a gradual system of competition in elementary dressage. There are classes for beginning horses and riders, then medium and advanced dressage, and jumping classes. Of course, jumping and three-day-event horses do not usually go beyond elementary or occasionally medium dressage.

Chapter III

The Seat and Aids of the Rider

The rider obtains the foundation of a good and a secure seat from the correct fundamental exercises and the steady practice of them as discussed in this chapter. Once a rider has achieved a secure seat and has learned the proper aids, he can further develop his seat into a driving seat by bracing his back and using the leg aids properly and thereby influencing the horse's movements. The driving seat has to be predominant in all gaits and paces. From the beginning, the rider should give the utmost attention to his *driving* seat, so that he uses the seat to drive (or push) the horse forward. The forward driving seat is important—it enables the rider to control the horse more effectively on the flat, over jumps, cross-country, and in the execution of dressage figures. The driving seat will also enable the rider to train his horse and to school himself in his chosen field should he desire to enter competition and represent his country in International and Olympic events. Again, a driving seat is strengthened by steady practice of figures or exercises, and also by cross-country riding and jumping. Any sincerely interested rider can achieve this seat. The young riders of

Mrs. Lois Stephens on *Ealkland,* demonstrating the correct seat. The correct seat enables the rider to execute the correct collected trot. Very good engagement of the horse's hindlegs makes it possible for the horse to erect himself. The visibility of the long neck muscle of the horse is proof of his lightness on the reins. Horse and rider are perfectly relaxed and balanced. *(Foto Mitschke.)*

the Pony Clubs and 4-H Clubs strengthen their driving seat by participation in eventing—jumping, cross-country riding, and dressage.

In the development of the rider's seat, attention should first be given to the rider's upper body. The rider should sit straight and his upper body should rest on the two seat bones. Whether riding on a straight line or on two-tracks, the upper body should *always* rest on the seat bones, and the horse's neck should be aligned with the middle of the rider's upper body. The rider, by bracing his back muscles, will be able to keep his own spine straight and firm. Regular inhaling and exhaling will prevent the rider from becoming stiff and tense. A hollow back is as wrong as a round back: both forms of posture prevent the rider from influencing the horse properly. It is of great importance that the rider relax his hip joints so that the inside of his legs, from the hip down, rest against the horse's sides in a *natural* position. Relaxed hip joints will keep the rider's upper body balanced. The knees should be bent and held low, just touching the horse's sides. The lower part of the rider's legs should gently but steadily touch the horse's sides. The rider's toes should be raised so that his leg muscles are tight—this will enable him to influence the horse's hind legs with the necessary pressure. The toe should not be turned too much to the inside or too much to the outside. When the rider's leg rests against the horse in a natural position, the toes will be turned in the proper position. Turning the toe too much to the inside will make it difficult for the rider to keep correct leg contact with the horse's side. Turning the toe too much to the outside will make it impossible for the rider to keep in contact with his knees.

The rider should maintain a relaxed but secure seat at all times. A secure seat is achieved by riding often without stirrups. In the beginning, this must be practiced for a short time, gradually increasing the length

Miss Rosalie Stecken on *Irish Faith* (Saddlebred), demonstrating the straight seat.

Miss Julie Walsh on *Hank* (Halfbred), demonstrating the forward seat. Second in the National Pony Club Rally, 1972.

of time during each practice session. The rider will soon have a steady and firm leg position. Looking at the rider from the side, one should be able to draw a straight line through the rider's shoulder, hip, and heel (this indicates that the rider is sitting properly). Through daily riding and practice the rider will begin to develop the steady, firm legs necessary to make the horse sensitive and responsive to the leg aids. Unsteady legs will make the horse dull to the leg aids. The rider should grip the horse with his calves. To further strengthen his leg muscles, the rider should participate in sports in which these muscles are used—for example, hiking, bicycling, and swimming. Riders who follow this advice will discover how helpful these sports are in developing and strengthening the muscles necessary to drive the horse forward or side-forward. Only from a correct seat is the rider able to give the proper and invisible aids. *The seat is correct when the rider can drive his horse vigorously forward step-by-step and stride-by-stride.*

The rider must use the following aids to influence the horse's hind legs, which are used for the forward impulsion of every horse. When the rider bends the horse around his inside leg, his outside leg, held back slightly, will influence the outside hind leg of the horse to step sideward and forward. The rider will then feel that the horse contracts his inside back muscle by expanding the outside muscle. This also will result in the correct bending of the horse's neck with relatively little influence of the hands. The rider must also learn to feel when the horse's hind legs lift off the ground. The contraction of the left or right back muscle indicates that the left or the right hind leg is in the air. This is the moment when the rider can best influence the horse to step more forward or sideward.

To increase the gait or pace, the rider must apply pressure with both legs. This is also done in executing half-halts and full halts, and in backing at an even pace. (To achieve the half-halt the rider applies pressure with both legs, thereby pushing the horse forward onto the bit which causes him to yield to the rider's fixed hands.) It is important for the horse *always* to be relaxed; then the increase or decrease of the gaits or paces will be supple and smooth. The aids the rider has to give for half-halts need to be practiced frequently until the rider has a feeling for coordinating his aids. The rider has to give half-halts riding on single- or two-tracks; in ordinary, strong, collected, or extended gaits; before the corners; before all turning figures; and prior to increasing or decreasing the gaits and paces. Only a horse which responds to these aids will be easy for the rider to guide, and only then will the horse be able to relax and to be balanced.

The rider's back is also an aid and plays a most important part in training the horse or competing in dressage classes. The rider must be able to tighten and relax his back muscles according to the amount of impulsion he needs to influence the horse. The rider must use a braced back to assist his legs to apply pressure to achieve the utmost impulsion from his horse. Only a rider who can tighten and relax his back muscles whenever necessary is able to influence his horse in the proper way. This alone is decisive in determining the good or bad performance of the horse. This will push the horse onto the bit, which will assist the rider's fixed hands to decrease the gaits or paces of the horse and will maintain the regularity and impulsion of the horse. As soon as the rider feels his horse yield to his fixed hands, he can lighten his hands and keep his horse balanced and relaxed. A relaxed horse will let the rider feel the swinging up and down motion of his spine, and the rider will learn to feel the contraction and expansion of the horse's back muscles. A relaxed horse will enable the rider to relax and sit comfortably in the saddle. The rider must practice for a long time without stirrups until he achieves the technique of coordinating his aids. He will feel the horse respond willingly and sensitively to the use of his back as a lever to the horse's back motion.

The rider will easily achieve the feeling for and coordination of his aids at a reduced momentum—the working walk or working trot (sitting), and in the working canter. The rider must use the driving aids to urge the horse's hind legs to step forward briskly to the rider's fixed hands. Every horse, feeling the pressure on the bit, will yield to the rider's hands and will become light on the bit. The rider will achieve this action easily by much riding on a circle. Once the horse and rider have progressed to this point, the rider can practice more turning figures—first at a walk. Besides the repetition of riding circles, the rider should practice figure eights, serpentines, and smaller circles until he can guide the horse in a volt (the smallest circle on one track). The rider should be certain that his hands are fixed and not pulling backwards.

The rider's hands are of secondary importance. The rider should only take (fixed hands) or give (relaxed hands). The hands should *never* be used in backing the horse; that is, pulling back on the reins. This will cause resistance on the horse's part. The rider should position the back of his hands and lower arms so that they are *parallel* to the ground with thumbs uppermost and so that a straight line can be drawn from the elbow through the wrist to the snaffle ring.

A horse should not be punished because he resists the rider's commands. This resistance indicates that the horse has not yet developed the necessary flexibility, and therefore needs more figure work and appropriate exercises. When the horse resists, the rider should hold his hands three to four hands apart. He should then apply pressure with the inside leg to urge the inside hind leg of the horse to step more under the horse's body and between the horse's front legs. The rider will feel the horse discontinue the resistance and yield to the rider's leg; the horse will become light on the rider's hands. This must be practiced in both directions. When the horse continues to resist, the rider should raise his hands two or three hands higher and hold them two or three hands apart. The rider then can use his back to push his hips forward in the saddle which will push the horse forward onto the bit and cause the horse to yield to the rider's hands. These aids are very effective and should only be used temporarily. If this is *patiently* done, the rider can avoid fighting his horse by hitting, kicking, or jerking. The rider should do this work gradually so that the horse accepts these aids. Otherwise, the rider will be the loser because of the greater physical strength of the horse.

In the straight and forward seats, the rider will be able to influence his horse only by coordination of the appropriate aids (hands, legs, weight) which are of great importance because they will enable him to properly influence the horse to jump, to go cross-country, or to go through a dressage test. The strength of these aids depends entirely on the horse's sensitivity and his training. For this reason, under no circumstances can the rider neglect his seat. He must constantly bear in mind that only through the correct seat is he able to influence the horse properly to relax and to maintain his balance in daily work, especially when the horse resists. Only when the horse is relaxed and balanced is he able to remain on the aids and to accept them.

Once the rider begins eventing or jumping, he must use the forward seat. (In the forward seat the rider must shorten the stirrups two notches [holes] and incline his shoulders forward according to the speed of the horse and the height of the jump. His weight must be in the stirrups, and his upper body must be balanced at the knee joint.)

All figures in dressage tests are fundamentally the same. These figures are: crossing the full or half ring, or crossing over the center line to change direction; changing hands by changing through or out of the circle; riding serpentines along the long side or from one side to the other; and the smallest turn on one track—the volt. The volt is the utmost a horse is able to bend evenly from poll to tail. The rider should be able to guide his horse with his back and legs through all of these figures.

A rider should be asked only for ordinary and strong gaits in a 66 by 132 foot arena for the lower level tests so that he can keep his horse on the aids. It will be evident that the horse is on the aids if he is relaxed, in balance, and proceeds with brisk forward impulsion and a light connection between his mouth and the rider's hands. Also, it will be evident that the horse is on the aids if the rider rides through all corners and figures with great accuracy.

A well-trained horse which is flexible and relaxed responds quickly to the increasing and decreasing aids and gives the impression that he is working on his own. This permits the rider to relax and sit comfortably in the saddle. Also, a well-trained horse needs only very light aids. The rider who can guide his horse with invisible aids and light contact between his hands and the horse's mouth can be assured that his horse is relaxed and well-balanced. In addition, a well-trained horse, under a rider with a correct seat, will go willingly and sensibly through all the figures, and will shorten and lengthen his base of support by shortening and lengthening his steps and strides, thereby performing tests A and B well. These tests are the basic requirements of the Pony Clubs.

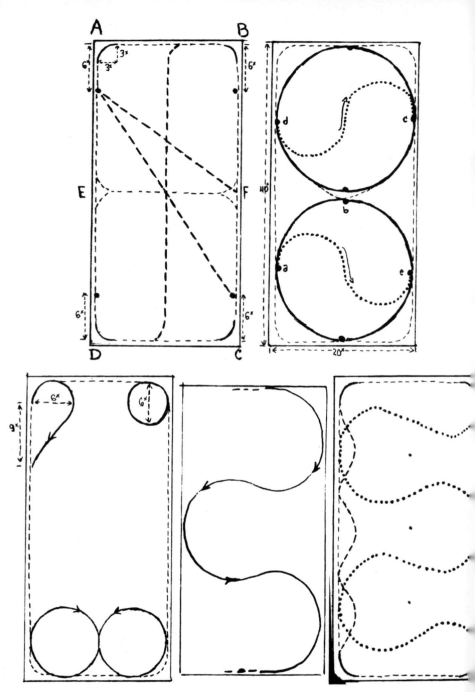

The fundamental figures.

One very important fact should be mentioned here: A rider who has the asset of a slender, long-legged body (thus creating an attractive appearance on the horse) will not necessarily be a better rider than one with a heavier physique or shorter legs.

It must also be mentioned that riders who use the forward seat will find that their horses can be hunted, jumped, or evented much more easily, because their horses will be sensitive and responsive to the rider's aids and will stay balanced and relaxed.

Strong Trot.

Chapter IV

The Gaits and Paces of the Horse

Since the founding of the F.E.I. there has been confusion about the gaits and paces in the lower level tests. There are also many conflicting opinions on the development of the collected and extended gaits. Every rider who wants to compete in International and Olympic competition has to bear in mind that a horse can only shorten or lengthen his base of support. The difference lies in the *impression* the horse is able to give in performing these gaits and paces. Only a relaxed and balanced horse is able to lengthen his steps and strides while maintaining the same rhythm, and for this reason it is important for the horse and rider to first perfect the ordinary and strong paces in all gaits.

The rider must develop the power of the horse's hind legs to push. Every horse, according to his natural way of moving, will show relaxation, balance, harmony, and grace in his movements. The rider must be able to feel the swinging up and down motion of the horse's spine and also the contraction and expansion of the horse's back muscles. He must sit comfortably by driving his horse vigorously forward. The horse will move with a more forward and upward motion of his legs

Strong Walk.

Collected Trot.

through the forward thrust of his hind legs. In this way the rider can train his horse to undulate with both hind legs in brisk and regular forward gaits and paces. The undulation must be visible, especially in the collected and extended gaits on single- and two-tracks. This is correctly stated in one book as: "the load must be evenly distributed on the horse's legs." The rider can avoid unevenness with both hind legs in the sequence of all gaits and paces. The Advisory Committee expressed this differently in *Notes on Dressage* by stating that the horse's hind hooves must step in the prints of the forehand in ordinary and collected gaits on the single- or two-tracks.* If the rider bears this in mind, he can avoid undue hardship for himself and his horse. The rider should not interfere with his hands, as this only provokes resistance and disobedience in the horse.

After the rider has his horse trained and perfected in the ordinary and strong paces in all gaits, he can start to train his horse for the collected and extended paces by giving the horse exercises on two-tracks. These two-track exercises culminate in the counterchanges to the left and right from the centerline, also known as the zig-zag traverse. Through these exercises every horse has to bend the hip and hock joints more. The horse will then lower his croup and lighten his front legs by using his extensor and flexor muscles more actively. The combined power of the horse's hind legs to push and to carry will give the horse the possibility of moving more upward and forward with his legs. This is known as cadence. It is a pronounced, rhythmical movement in the beat of the collected and extended paces in all gaits. Cadence is the difference between ordinary and strong and collected and extended paces. Cadence cannot be judged by time and distance, but only by the impression the horse is able to give to the

*See excerpts from *Notes on Dressage*, page 192.

Extended Trot.

Collected Canter.

judge. The relaxed and balanced horse can be trained—through shortening and lengthening the base of support and riding all exercises on two-tracks—to find cadence by himself. Riders who do not pay enough attention to the horse's relaxation and the sequence of the gaits in all paces make it difficult for themselves to train their horses and make it difficult for the horses to be obedient.

It is essential for the rider to teach his horse to accept the legs. Leg-yielding with the inside and outside leg teaches the horse to yield to the legs and also to move sideward in the sequence of the walk and trot, but should be done mostly at the walk. Our interested riders must bear in mind that the horse must first learn to respond to the rider's legs, and also that the horse must learn to go on two-tracks with his front and hind legs. The rider is able to train his horse through leg-yielding by guiding his horse through all the fundamental figures on a single-track using the influence of his driving seat; that is, mainly with his legs and back and with relatively little use of his hands. In this way, the rider will be able to maintain the proper sequence in all gaits and paces. If the rider trains his horse to the highest degree of longitudinal and lateral flexibility, the horse must still maintain the same sequence in the gaits and paces. He can shorten the base of support to turn around his haunches in the walk and canter to perform the pirouette, and can trot in place to perform the piaffe. He can also lengthen his base of support to perform the extended gaits to the utmost. Riders must keep in mind that only the driving seat can maintain the sequence in all the gaits and paces. The driving aids have to be predominant whether shortening or lengthening the horse's base of support. Only then will the horse keep his back muscles relaxed so that his back will swing gently up and down. The horse can then use his hind legs freely and they can energetically

Shoulder-in.

and elastically thrust him off the ground with great impulsion, moving harmoniously and gracefully forward. In this way, the horse is able to carry himself and can maintain a light and steady connection between his mouth and the rider's hands. The rider should abstain from drilling his horse in the confinement of an indoor or outdoor ring. He should perfect all the gaits and paces by riding on the bridlepath where the terrain is level enough for shortening and lengthening the base of support. This is evidenced when the horse performs with relaxation, balance, and impulsion, and with a gently swinging back.

Horses with dragging hind legs (so-called "daisy cutters") are less suitable, although such horses can be trained to the highest level. Horses with natural balance, a natural thrust with the hind legs, and natural shoulder freedom are not only more promising but also more enjoyable to train. In the end this factor is decisive in *how* the horse expresses himself in all figures, gaits, and paces. For this reason our instructors and riders should bear in mind that they must not disturb the sequence of the gaits of the horse.

In the first stage of training, the rider must develop the power of the horse's hind legs to push forward energetically, while he is relaxed and balanced. All figures on a single-track and many transitions shortening and lengthening the base of support are very helpful in training the horse. For this reason it is advisable to start in the first stage with leg-yielding so that the horse learns to respond to the rider's legs. In the second stage, through use of all two-track exercises, the rider will be able to train the horse to become more flexible in the hip and hock joints; through this the croup is lowered and the front legs lightened. This, as well as transitions shortening and lengthening the base of support, makes it possible for the horse to move in a more pronounced, rhythmical movement in

Extended Trot. Note high croup, insufficient bending of hock and hip joints, head and neck too low, exaggerated stretching of the front leg (goose-stepping), and disharmony of the horse's movement.

Extended Trot (Arabian).

the beat of the collected and extended gaits and paces: in other words, in cadence.

In the end, a horse can perform the F.E.I. tests relaxed, balanced, and with great impulsion and accuracy. The horse must be able to maintain the sequence in the gaits and paces whether shortening or lengthening his base of support. The horse is then longitudinally and laterally flexible. Riders who observe the horse's nature will be successful. The best and the most enjoyable way to achieve it is to ride often outdoors in the country.

> Nature can live without art,
> but art cannot live without nature.

The training of a horse must follow this line of thought. From the beginning of the horse's training, riders and instructors must realize that it is of vital importance not to disturb the sequence of the horse's gaits in the walk, trot, and canter. Regardless of the use of the horse—jumping, eventing, or riding gaits and paces in the prescribed tests—he must be able to shorten and lengthen his steps and strides. A rider who pays attention to the horse's relaxation and balance will find the whole training progress more enjoyable than a rider who neglects the horse's nature.

The rider must strengthen the horse's muscles from the beginning so that the horse is able to flex his joints, especially the joints in his hindquarters. Exercises like riding figures, jumping over low obstacles or cavalletti, and riding cross-country are the means to this end. Through the exercises, every horse will become more supple and flexible. A well-trained horse will respond willingly, and in due progress will become very sensitive.

Horses with great ability to jump or great boldness in jumping in any terrain, or with a great way of mov-

Working trot and canter on a loose rein. Riding with loose reins allows the horse to stretch and the rider to strengthen the horse's muscles.

ing in the three gaits, are exceptional. As a rule, horses need training in shortening and lengthening their base of support to make it easy for the rider to guide them. For this reason, the rider should start the training on a very low level and ask progressively more according to the degree of improvement in the horse's suppleness and flexibility. For every horse and rider it will then be easier to jump higher, ride over more difficult terrain, or to perform gaits and figures in which a horse needs greater longitudinal and lateral flexibility. From the beginning, the rider must bear in mind that if he wants to compete in International or Olympic competition in dressage his horse has to be trained to the highest degree of suppleness and flexibility. To achieve this, the rider has to be able to make his horse sensitive and responsive to his driving aids. The more a horse must shorten his base of support, the more the rider has to influence the horse in order to maintain the balance and impulsion needed to be able to perform in a higher level in jumping, eventing, or riding intricate figures. The horse's muscles have to be strengthened and his joints made more flexible.

For a future dressage rider, an understanding of the gaits and paces is of great importance, and for every other rider jumping or eventing above the Pony Club requirements, it is a great help. In starting a horse at the beginning, the rider teaches his horse to carry weight and teaches the aids the rider wishes his horse to know in order to carry out the signals the rider uses. The most important aid the horse learns is to go forward when the rider squeezes his legs. By giving with the hands, a horse will walk; by taking with the hands and keeping the legs relatively passive, the horse learns to make a full stop. Through repetition every horse learns these simple aids quickly, and also learns to stay square on all four feet. In the same way, a horse learns to trot and to go back to a walk and to the full stop. After the horse gets used to this, the rider should ride in a big circle. Many horses will learn to canter simply by the rider moving his outside leg slightly back.

After the rider is able to stabilize his horse in the three gaits, the horse can be worked easily and will work willingly for the rider. *These are known as the working gaits.* This stabilizing of the horse in the gaits and making him go forward on the rider's legs is the first and foremost aid a horse learns. As soon as a horse is used to the rider's weight he will relax and will drop his head and neck forward and downward from the withers. Every horse will show this trait, regardless of his origin or breed. The rider can then feel the horse's mouth by taking the reins so that he can have a connection between his hands and the horse's mouth. The rider should never use his hands to force the horse to give to this connection. It must come by itself through the horse's natural way of moving—from the back to the front.

If the rider has patiently worked his horse in the three working gaits, the horse will go relaxed and balanced. The rider is then able to ride his horse with the reins in one hand. The rider should do this throughout the whole training program to convince himself that he has, through all the exercises in the different gaits and paces, achieved the flexibility and suppleness necessary for every horse and especially for a Grand Prix dressage horse.

After the rider has stabilized his horse in the three gaits every horse will find, by himself and through his relaxation and balance, the regularity and impulsion necessary for the ordinary gaits. The rider can then introduce his horse to all the fundamental figures. From the beginning, the rider should keep in mind that he should first ride larger figures, like circles, because the smaller a figure is the more difficult it is for the horse.

The figures should be ridden first in the ordinary walk. The rider should always keep in mind that he has to develop the power of the horse's hind legs to push. This is evidenced when the horse's hind legs step in the footprints of the front feet in the walk and trot. In the canter the horse should reach forward with the inside hind leg as much as possible in order to be able to canter in a calm, relaxed, and balanced manner. Through the ordinary gaits, leg-yielding, and the exercises in the figures on a single-track, every horse will become more supple and flexible in the hip joints, spine, ribs, and neck. To improve the horse's suppleness and flexibility the rider can start to train his horse to accept the half-halt by squeezing his legs, bracing his back, and fixing his hands. As soon as the rider feels the response from the horse he must relax his own muscles.

In the strong gaits, the horse should only lengthen the base of support. He should not go faster. The ability to shorten and to lengthen the base of support improves every horse's suppleness and flexibility. A horse is then able to keep his relaxation, balance, and the same rhythm in the ordinary and strong paces. This is very helpful for the requirements of the Pony Club rider. For every rider who wants to compete above the requirements of the Pony Clubs, it is a *necessity*.

The rider can develop the collected and extended gaits through many transitions from the ordinary and strong gaits and from riding all exercises on two-tracks. Slowly, but progressively, the joints of the hind legs will become more supple and flexible. Riders who pay attention to the development of these gaits so that the horse maintains his relaxation will not have great difficulties in improving the horse in this endeavor. All these exercises improve the horse's longitudinal and lateral flexibility. Every horse will slowly use his power to push, combined with the power of his hind legs to carry, by bending his hip and hock joints more. The rider can be effective only when he rides the horse in the shoulder-in, haunches in-and-out exercises so that his horse does not cross his legs as in leg-yielding. The horse's inside hind leg must follow the outside front leg, or the outside hind leg must follow the inside front leg, *without crossing.* From the side it looks like the horse is crossing his legs, but from the front one can observe that the horse sets the inside legs in front of the outside legs without crossing. Only in this way can any rider maintain the impulsion and influence the horse to bend the joints at his hindquarters to go in cadence. This enables the horse to lower the croup, erect himself, and lighten the forehand. The reflex motion of the extensor and flexor muscle makes it possible for the horse to show a pronounced beat in the collected and extended gaits. The collected and extended gaits are evidenced by the horse's moving forward energetically and elastically, with cadenced steps and strides. Harmonious and graceful steps and strides are evidence of proper training. Horses which show shortening of the neck and exaggerated steps, or which move with the hind legs apart, are under tension. Relaxation, balance, and vigorous forward impulsion have to be clearly visible while shortening and lengthening the base of support. If a horse steps well under his and the rider's body in the collected gaits, on single- or two-tracks, he still must step with his hind hooves in the direction of the front legs. Only then will the horse lower his croup by bending his hip and hock joints and be able to perform in cadence. For this reason, the F.E.I. has decided, in the latest rules, to seat three of the judges on the sidelines to make this more easily visible.

Chapter V

Stage I–The Teaching Period

In training a young horse for the lower level tests, the horse must first be made longitudinally and laterally supple. *He is made longitudinally supple by working on the straight at ordinary and strong gaits, preferably outdoors over varied terrain, and over cavalletti and low jumps. He is made laterally supple by walking, trotting, and cantering briskly in large circles and with leg-yielding exercises.*

The rider must be certain to keep the horse's body in a straight line when going straight ahead, and bent slightly but evenly the entire length of the spine when working in a circle. His front and hind prints must be in the same track in all this work. It is important to push the horse forward strongly at all times, even in the slower gaits, so that he exercises and stretches his muscles to the utmost, maintains an elegant posture, and keeps a steady, regular tempo. In this tempo the rider can work his horse to find the horse's balance in the walk, trot, and canter. At the walk and trot the horse's hind hooves must reach the footprints of the front hooves, so that the horse learns to use his hind legs to push by bending his hip joint.

This work, and all practice work up to and including the International standard, should be done with a snaffle bit. The double bridle is permitted in the more advanced tests to make it easier for horse and rider to work with invisible aids. The dropped noseband, when properly adjusted, is the most satisfactory for training horses. It should be applied four fingers above the top of the nostril and should be loose enough to permit two fingers to be placed easily between the noseband and the horse's nose. When used in this way it cannot hurt the horse unless he opens his mouth wide. He learns very soon to keep his mouth closed and to chew gently on the bit. The dropped noseband prevents the horse from getting his tongue over the bit, twisting his lower jaw from side to side, and developing other annoying habits. If the horse does not have problems and has a good mouth, the English noseband is preferred.

All this brisk elementary training develops a lithe, balanced horse. Litheness means that all the muscles are relatively equal in looseness and strength. Balance is a state of continuous equilibrium. Whether the horse moves fast or slow; forward, backward, or to the side; on the flat, over jumps, or cross-country; he is either *in balance* or *out of balance.*

The rider who prepares carefully and painstakingly for the first dressage test is like the wise man who built his house on a rock, for the beginning tests represent the foundation for all other work up to the Olympic standard. The emphasis is on doing seemingly simple things well.

When the young horse goes satisfactorily at the walk, trot and canter—which can be developed easily with the outside leg and outside rein—it is an easy matter to change from one circle to the other (like a large figure eight). The next step is to practice serpentines with large, regular loops. It is very important to make symmetrical curves and circles because these are gymnastic exercises for the horse. If the horse is inclined to make oval circles, it means that he is not supple enough to bend steadily and evenly, and that the rider is not pushing him forward enough.

Most of the ring work at the trot should be done without stirrups for three reasons. First, it is easier for the horse, particularly for one not far along in his training, to maintain his balance in turning figures. Second, it is easier for the rider to push him forward in the precise, brisk rhythm which is the secret of developing his muscles longitudinally. Third, sitting the trot is excellent practice for the rider in obtaining a firm, deep seat in all gaits, paces, and figures.

The deep seat most useful to the rider in training the horse is one in which the rider sits straight but supple, not stiff, exactly in the middle of the saddle, and goes smoothly with the movements of the horse. The upper body should rest firmly on the pelvis. Too much forward inclination would place the rider too much on his thighs; too much backward inclination would bring the knees of the rider too high. In both positions the rider is unable to influence the horse with his driving aids. The thighs, knees, and legs should be steady and well stretched downward. When the feet are hanging free the stirrup should strike slightly below the ankle bone. In the sitting trot the rider's seat should accurately follow the movements of the horse. A loose seat or bumping in the saddle is proof of stiffness in the rider's seat. At the canter, the rider should sit constantly in the saddle; his upper body should be steady and his shoulders must not be pushed back. The horse should be fitted with a sufficiently deep seated saddle; otherwise, it is impossible for the rider to hold a correct seat. All movements should be attained without apparent effort. Regular inhaling and exhaling by the rider is very important in order to maintain the proper posture.

Riding with the reins in one hand is proof of how supple and well balanced the horse is.

The seat is correct when the rider can continuously push his horse forward step by step and stride by stride through the influence of his back and legs, with light hands and steady contact with the horse's mouth. The influence of the aids should always be smooth and flexible: strong when necessary, but always invisible. With a well-trained horse, the rider's aids should not be visible—neither from his upper body, his legs, nor his hands. Under a rider with a good seat the horse will show calmness and steadiness at all gaits, paces, and figures. The rider should normally carry his hands one hand's height above the withers and two hands in front of his own body so that there is a nearly straight line from the rider's elbows to the rings of the snaffle.

When the rider posts at the trot, he should make a point of posting an equal amount of time on each diagonal. The rider must constantly bear in mind that he drives the horse with his outside leg. The rider must realize that only when the horse's outside hind leg is in the air can he push it forward vigorously with his own outside leg.

After introducing serpentines, the rider should start leg-yielding exercises. Regardless of the contention that leg-yielding is not used in classical riding or in executing figures, it is important to use this exercise in training the horse from the first level test to the Grand Prix level because it keeps the horse on the driving aids and teaches the horse to be responsive to the rider's legs.

Leg-yielding is the first exercise in which the horse learns to respond to the rider's lateral aids. On feeling the action of the rein the horse must yield and bend his neck. The same reaction applies to the pressure of the rider's leg; the horse must yield and bend his body around the rider's leg without pushing his weight

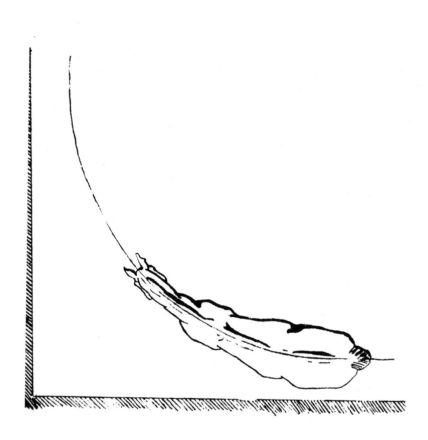

A correct corner.

against the rider's leg. The horse should move with hind legs and front legs in a 45-degree angle to the wall so that he crosses his legs.

It will be found that circles help in developing this first exercise in two-tracking, and as the leg-yielding progresses the horse will find it easier to execute perfect circles. Both exercises develop and supple the horse laterally. Leg-yielding especially supples the shoulder and hip joints so that they can move freely to the side and the horse can increase the bend in his spine and ribs.

Leg-yielding should be begun at a walk along a wall or fence. Riding on the right hand, for example, with the wall on the left, the rider bends the horse to the left around his left leg, pushing the horse strongly forward and sideward so that the horse must cross his legs. This should be done for only two or three steps at first. The horse is then ridden strongly forward. This should be practiced in both directions. The rider will find that one side is easier than the other. Continued work on circles, serpentines, and leg-yielding while on the circles will help to bring the horse to a state of lateral flexibility where he will respond with ease to leg-yielding. The leg-yielding exercise must always be followed by vigorous riding straight ahead. The rider must not allow himself to become so absorbed in the ring exercises that he neglects riding outdoors, since this is essential to the horse in all stages of his training.

As the horse becomes more proficient, leg-yielding with the inside leg, that is, with the horse's head away from the wall, can be begun. Later, when this also is easy for the horse, leg-yielding both ways can be done at the trot. Whether at the walk or trot, the rider must watch that the horse does not fall out of correct balance and that he maintains vigor and regularity.

One other figure, the turn on the forehand, belongs in the beginning stage. This is another exercise in bending the horse laterally. While riding along a wall the horse is brought to a halt on the bit. The rider bends him slightly to the outside (toward the wall) and with his outside leg encourages the horse to turn, pivoting the hindquarters around the forehand. Guard against any tendency of the horse to step backward; in the beginning it does not matter if the horse moves forward. The rider can avoid any tendency to move forward by giving half-halts. If the horse steps backward it means the rider is influencing the horse too much with his hands, and the horse should be ridden vigorously straight ahead before the exercise is tried again.

The halt and backing should also be practiced. In the halt, the horse is pushed strongly with back and legs into the rider's fixed hands which do not yield until the horse yields, relaxes his jaw, and stands quietly and square. This should not be asked in the lower level tests as long as the horse does not step backward after he is brought to a full halt. The rider's legs must keep contact with the horse's sides, and the horse must remain in balance on the bit. As the rider relaxes his fingers, the horse must slowly and gently chew the bit out of the rider's hands, stretching his neck forward and downward until the reins slip through the rider's fingers to the buckle. This is a very important exercise for the horse. It is proof of his relaxation and his ability to stretch his muscles. A horse which is tense or nervous will not "chew the reins out of the rider's hands," but will jerk them impatiently or remain with his head held stiffly in the air. This exercise can and should be done in the working gaits, even over low jumps.

The rider should practice the exercises of the half-halt and the halt frequently to allow the horse to stretch his neck and back muscles, and also to make sure that he is relaxed and on the bit. The rider must never throw the reins down at the halt or while in motion, but must wait for the horse to chew them gently,

Correct backing.

in a relaxed manner, out of his hands. The rider must
not forget to allow the horse to stretch in this manner
in the walk, trot, and canter. The half-halt is given by
pushing the horse with back and legs into the bit, and
the horse must yield to the rider's fixed hands. *The
half-halt has to be given by the rider to get the attention
of the horse in order to maintain balance and to de-*

crease the gaits even before asking the horse to make a full stop or to back up.

Backing is an exercise much abused and overdone. In backing, the rider first halts as described above, without letting the reins slip through his fingers. He then urges the horse forward with legs and back, without yielding his fixed hands. The horse will step backward, still in balance and on the bit. The backing must be straight, calm, and regular, as in moving forward. If the horse is inclined to get behind the bit, backing must be discontinued for some time. When the horse is first exercised in backing, only one or two steps must be asked, followed by brisk trotting forward. Backing should be practiced only a few times in each lesson to avoid the horse's anticipating the execution of this exercise.

As the horse becomes supple enough to make perfect circles and serpentines easily, the rider may commence volts (or volten) at the walk and trot, and last at the canter. These are circles of 20 feet in diameter, usually done at a specific place while riding along a wall, and they may later be done in a series of perhaps two or three on the long side of the riding hall. Be certain that the horse's hind and front footprints stay in the same track, that he maintains his regularity, that he stays gently and evenly on the bit—not pulling toward left or right—and remains in balance. If the horse is inclined to lean on the outside rein, the rider should correct this by bending the horse to the outside.

Up to now we have said nothing about turning the corners of the ring. This in itself is an exercise which can count for or against the horse in National or International competition. When the horse is laterally flexible enough to start volts, the rider can begin practicing correct corners. The horse must be kept close to the wall and ridden right into the corner without cutting across, thus marking each corner like a quarter volt. An easy way to begin is to make volts in the corners first. This accustoms the horse to staying close to the wall. It should be done first at the walk, then at the trot, and last at the canter. *The rider must have the horse well on his aids to do this and should call the horse to attention with a half-halt just as they approach the corner.*

Another exercise which requires the rider's careful practice is the transition between gaits and between paces in the same gait. Here again, a good foundation will pay off in the more advanced dressage tests. Each transition must be clearly evident at the exact point when it is required—this step is ordinary trot, next step is strong trot—or whatever the test demands or whatever the rider demands of his horse in practice. Transitions are easiest to make in the corners of the ring. When the rider brings his horse to attention and rides well into the corner, he is then perfectly balanced, most alert, and attentive to the rider's aids. Therefore, he will respond instantly to a request to change pace or gait. In practicing transitions, one should first make them in corners, as mentioned above; for example, ordinary trot on the short side, strong trot on the long side, and so forth around the ring. When, after many practice sessions, the horse performs well in this way, the rider may ask for transitions at other points. As in all training, the rider must try to avoid having the horse anticipate the commands.

The horse which is trained in exercises for the beginning tests may be a future hunter, jumper, cross-country, hack, or potential advanced dressage horse. Whatever the rider's hopes or plans for the horse, at this stage most of his work should be done outdoors, over bridlepaths, and cross-country. He should be jumped over low jumps (not more than two feet) three times a week.

The large muscles in the horse's back are his most important muscles. They control his forehand, hindquarters, and neck. A horse with a stiff back will be stiff all over, as any human who has experienced a touch of lumbago will agree. In the supple horses, the back muscles will swing gently as the horse moves. The sensitive rider with a firm seat will be able to feel how the horse's back is stiff when he first comes from the stable, and can tell when he begins to become limber. The rider will also feel the difference between an untrained horse, one which has been incorrectly trained, and a horse which has had training in the correct, natural way.

Most of the exercises described in this chapter can and should be practiced while riding cross-country. Circles and volts can be ridden in flat fields; transitions and leg-yielding can be practiced while riding along fences or walls; halts and backing can be practiced everywhere. It is of utmost importance to keep the horse moving at brisk, free, regular gaits. This is to develop the horse's power to push himself and the rider forward. Again, the rider must be sure that the horse's body is straight when going straight ahead, and evenly bent when executing curved figures. It is also important to maintain the horse's light, balanced carriage, and to keep him on the rider's aids. The rider has to frequently give half-halts to maintain this. Up to this point the rider has taught the horse to respond in a very simple way to his legs, weight, and hands. The horse has learned to carry his rider in a relaxed and balanced manner indoors or outdoors, cross-country and over low jumps, under English, Western or Sidesaddle. The horse is obedient and a necessary foundation is laid.

Chapter VI

Schooling Over Cavalletti and Grid

by General Jonathan R. Burton

General Jonathan R. Burton, a combat veteran of World War II, went into Leyte on D-Day and saw action in Luzon, Manila, and Tokyo. Following the war he served as an instructor in Advanced Horsemanship at the Cavalry School and on the U.S. Army Equestrian Team. He has shown horses at major shows in Europe and the United States. As a member of the USET he participated in three day events in London (1948) and Stockholm (1956). Gen. Burton is a Senior Judge and Steward of the American Horse Show Association and as such has judged major shows at Madison Square Garden, Harrisburg, Houston, Colorado Springs, Pebble Beach and Washington, D.C. He has given freely of his time to young people as Governor of the U. S. Pony Clubs and conducted numerous clinics on horsemanship and dressage.

The word cavalletti is Italian—literally translated, it means "little jumps." If you look for it in your unabridged dictionary or encyclopedia, it is not to be found. Baranowski, in his *International Horseman's Dictionary*, gives us a picture of one simple type of cavalletti, and indicates that the name is the same in English, French, and German (although the Germans also have the alternative name *Bodenrick*), all of which makes it apparent that this is a technical term of interest only to horsemen. Originally, cavalletti was the name applied to very small obstacles used by Italian horsemen either singly or, more commonly, in multiple combinations primarily for schooling young horses.

The technique of schooling over cavalletti was soon found to be extremely flexible, suitable for many different uses, and easily varied in form, depending on the purpose for which it is being used. Of special interest to Pony Club instructors is its usefulness as a method of instruction for the rider.

Used in its simplest form, and with an old horse well schooled over cavelletti and a novice rider, cavalletti may be solely a convenient method of introducing our novice to jumping. The minute we go beyond this stage, the use of the cavalletti, like most other methods of instruction, becomes both a device for teaching the rider and for training and improving the horse. Indeed, if cavalletti is not used in a manner calculated to benefit both the horse and the rider, the instructor is not making proper use of the tools at his command. Accordingly, if we are working along proper lines, we will be improving the performance and the abilities of both horse and rider.

If you have never seen or heard of cavalletti, you might at this point say "What are these little jumps you call cavalletti, what do they look like, and how little are they?" Well, to answer the last question first, they can be and often are very little indeed. A pole or small log lying on the ground is cavalletti in its simplest form. Actually, this is the form in which we should first present cavalletti to the untrained horse or to the novice rider. At this stage, we are *not* seeking to obtain even a little jump. In the case of the horse, we want him to lower his head and neck, look where he is going, and calmly walk and later trot over the obstacle. And in the case of the rider, we are at this point seeking only to have him approach, ride over, and leave this little obstacle, calmly, quietly, and in proper position. For this purpose, this simple form of cavalletti—poles or logs placed on the ground—is not only adequate but is preferable to the raised type of cavalletti which is used for some of the more advanced work to be described later.

Perhaps at this point it is also appropriate to describe the form which our cavalletti may take and the manner in which they may be constructed. As already stated, simple poles laid on the ground are quite adequate for certain uses. The length of the poles (establishing the width of the jump) should be at least eight feet and preferably longer—up to twelve feet. The longer poles are preferable, but are heavier and more cumbersome to handle. The diameter should be at least four inches. A smaller diameter pole is often not easily seen, especially if placed on heavy turf. A larger diameter is entirely satisfactory except for the added weight and the corresponding increased burden in handling.

Simple poles constructed without any base or crosspiece have the disadvantage that they are very easily disarranged or knocked out of position when, as frequently happens, a horse hits, drags his toe, or stumbles over the poles. This disadvantage is not important if an instructor or an assistant is dismounted and can replace the poles as they are knocked out of position. On the other hand, a rider using cavalletti, when no dismounted assistant is available, will ordinarily wish to use poles mounted on endpieces so constructed that they will not be so readily rolled or knocked out of position. Some instructors prefer poles so constructed even when an assistant or dismounted instructor is available.

Many different methods of construction will suggest themselves to the ingenious jump builder. If the cavalletti are intended for use at the trot, the pole should not be raised to a height of more than six to eight inches. If the cavalletti are to be used for other purposes as described later in this chapter, a greater height may be required, but for most purposes, the height should not exceed 18 inches.

If your pupils have had some slight experience in jumping, it will be entirely appropriate to start directly with the methods which we are about to describe. However, if your pupils, or some of them, are complete novices at least in jumping, it is suggested that as a preliminary, and during ring instruction on several different days, poles be placed on the ground across the track at the edge of the ring—starting with only one pole and then adding others at random places around the track. Your pupils singly, and then as a group, will first walk and later trot over these poles on the ground. A galloping position suitable for the approach to a jump should be taught and emphasized during this preparatory work, but the horses should be permitted to move only at the trot, and every effort should be made to avoid even a slight hop as the horse moves over the pole. The goal is to have the horse trot over each pole quietly and completely in stride, and to have the pupil ride completely relaxed as if no poles were on the ground. When this has been accomplished, we leave the single poles (which are themselves a form of cavalletti) and turn to the grid of poles on the ground.

We start our instruction with a grid of seven heavy bars placed on the ground parallel to each other. If a ring or other enclosure is being used, the grid should ordinarily be placed more or less in the center and along the long axis of the ring. For later use, jump standards should be placed on each side of the bar at the far end of the ring. The grid will look something like this:

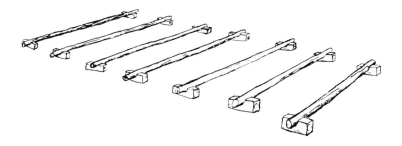

The first step in using the grid is to take the horse over the grid at the walk. Since the bars will be spaced for trotting, the horse may do this rather awkwardly, taking half strides and perhaps hitting or stumbling over the bars. This is all a part of getting him to lower his head and to look where he is going. Some horses will energetically resist being taken over the grid. A little patience and quiet handling will generally overcome this. Following another horse will help, and if difficulty persists, walk the horse from side to side through (rather than over) the bars.

The walking stage is simply to get the horse accustomed to the grid and to accept it without timidity or resistance. After passing over the grid, the horse should continue straight ahead for 30 or more feet, then circle in a sweeping turn to come back parallel to the grid, and when 30 or more feet beyond the beginning of the grid should again make a wide turn for a straight approach and another pass over the grid. After passing over the grid, the turns should be made alternately, one time to the left and the next time to the right.

When this has been accomplished satisfactorily at the walk (which will often be only after three or four passes over the grid), the horse is then ridden over the grid in the same manner at a medium speed trot. Here it becomes important to maintain a completely uniform pace, and particularly to keep the same speed over the grid as during the rest of the movement. If this is not readily accomplished, resume the preparatory work at a walk, and most important, do not stop and start. As long as you are practicing over the cavalletti, keep going at a uniform pace. Of course, this does not mean that you cannot discontinue your cavalletti work and then return to it later in the schooling period. But as long as the work is over the cavalletti, keep it going.

Up to this point we have presented the procedure from the standpoint of one horse and one rider. Actually, however, this work as we have described it can be practiced to great advantage by working as a group and going over the course in a column. Here the instructor must use judgment as to the order in which he places his horses and riders. Generally, it is best to have a strong rider on a reliable horse as the leader, but some horses who work quietly in front are difficult in the rear, so it may, on occasion, be necessary to place the difficult horse in front. This is important because we are aiming toward a quiet, relaxed ride for all members of the group. Be mindful also that other horses will work better over cavalletti if placed at the rear of the column. So in your effort to obtain a quiet, even performance, experiment with changes in the position of any horse whose performance is not satisfactory.

I have purposely said nothing, up to this point, about the distance or interval at which you should place the bars which make up the grid, since the importance of this spacing can perhaps be better understood having before you at least a preliminary picture of the use to be made of the grid and of the results which you are trying to achieve. As must now be apparent, the correct spacing or interval is important, indeed essential, if the horse is to travel smoothly and comfortably over the grid.

The correct spacing will vary greatly for different horses: for a small pony, perhaps as close as 3-1/2 feet; for a medium-sized, cold-blooded horse, perhaps as little as four feet; a big, free-striding horse may do his best with an interval of as much as six feet. Obviously, therefore, if your group includes horses of widely differing size and natural stride, it may be necessary to divide the group so that all the horses working at any one time can accommodate themselves to the same interval.

Your distance will also vary with the work you are doing and the extent to which the horses have achieved a calm, relaxed performance. Initially, and especially if the horses (or some of them) tend to heat up and to increase the tempo of the trot when going over the grid, the interval should be reduced somewhat. Later, when quietness and relaxation have been developed, the distance should be increased to the comfortable limit of the horses' stride to encourage an extension of the stride without any increase in tempo.

Obviously, these are general rules only. The correct distance at any given time can be determined only by observing the performance over the grid and adjusting the interval to accomplish the desired result.

Up to this point, we have described the use of cavalletti at this initial stage from the standpoint of the trainer seeking to obtain from the horse a calm, relaxed, even performance. This is so because not only at this initial stage but also to an even greater extent at the later stages, calmness and relaxation are essential to improvement not only for the horse but for the rider as well. Obviously, if we are introducing an inexperienced rider to jumping by the use of cavalletti, it is desirable that both this preparatory work and the work over jumps presently to be described should have been satisfactorily accomplished on the horse by a more experienced rider before our novice rider takes over. When this is not possible, quite good results can generally be obtained provided that the horse has had some jumping experience and is reasonably calm and provided that no effort is made to hurry the progress of the work, even if all the riding is done by our less experienced rider.

Now, what should our rider have been doing, or attempting to do? First, the horse must be under control. Under no circumstances is the horse to be permitted to canter over the grid. If the horse breaks into a canter, he should, if possible, be turned to the side and out of the grid. As control and calmness are achieved, the rider should take a lighter and lighter contact with the mouth, so that in due course the horse is permitted (if control allows) to pass over the cavalletti on a completely loose rein, starting preferably two or three strides before entering the grid. Prior to entering the grid, the rider should assume the forward position which would be used in approaching a jump. This is sometimes referred to as the galloping position, although in this instance it is a position to be assumed at the trot. It should be maintained through the grid and for two or three strides after leaving the grid.

As already indicated, this first stage is only preparatory to the later stages which are to follow. But it is a foundation without which the work at the later stages will not be productive. How long should this first stage take? There is no standard. I have accomplished a very creditable performance in 20 minutes. I have also worked every day for a week and even then, from the standpoint of calmness and relaxation, the performance left much to be desired. The only rule is: Don't hurry and don't go on to the second stage until you have a thoroughly satisfactory performance at the first stage.

So now we come to Stage Two. The next to the last bar is taken from the ground and placed on the jump standards over or perhaps a few inches on the far side of what was previously the last bar of the grid. The arrangement of the bars will now look like this:

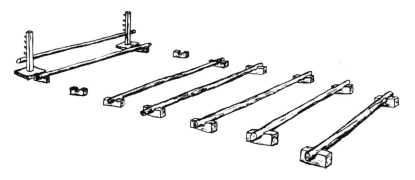

The initial height at which you place the bar will vary with the ability of both horse and rider, but a good rule is to start at the lowest height which will induce the horse to make a little hop over the bar. Perhaps this will be one foot, or perhaps 18 inches. It will certainly not be higher to start with than two feet. Err on the low side, not the high side. If you have a very green or timid horse or a very inexperienced rider, you may find it desirable to raise only one end of the bar until the horse (or the rider) becomes accustomed to going over the raised bar.

The procedure is exactly as before, that is, the pace will be a medium trot. If the horse canters after his little hop, he is quietly but quickly brought back to the trot.

The work continues, probably for two or more days, until the horse goes as quietly over the grid with the little hop at the end as he did when all the poles were on the ground. Then, if you started with a very low jump, gradually increase the height up to two feet.

What about our rider? He should ride exactly as he did when the poles were on the ground. He assumes a jumping position, preferably with loose reins, before entering the grid. He maintains this position through the grid, over the jump, and for two or three strides beyond. The jump becomes simply a part of the grid. He makes no special preparation for the jump, for he is already in a jumping position. And if not? Then obviously you go back to Stage One, for the rider has not yet learned to maintain his jumping position while riding through the grid, all of which emphasizes the importance of securing a completely satisfactory performance at Stage One before progressing to Stage Two. If the foundation work at Stage One is carried out correctly and for an adequate period of time, you will be gratified at how rarely even your novice jumper will be left behind when he is faced with his first little jump.

We will now assume you have come to the point where you are quite satisfied with the performance of both the horse and of the rider, at Stage Two. With inexperienced riders and schooled horses, this might come in the very first instruction period. With average pupils and average horses, it will probably come only after several instruction periods and plenty of work.

So now we come to Stage Three. For this, we pick up bar 3 and place it on the standards so that we now have a jump about 2-1/2 feet in height. You will also have an appreciable distance from the last remaining bar of the grid to the jump. For example, if your bars were spaced with a 4-1/2 foot interval, there will be a distance of about 14 feet. With this distance, and faced with a 2-1/2 foot jump, the horse will almost certainly put in one canter stride of his own accord before jumping. And so we have accomplished the transition to a jump from the canter, and over a more substantial obstacle. The grid and jump used at Stage Three will look like:

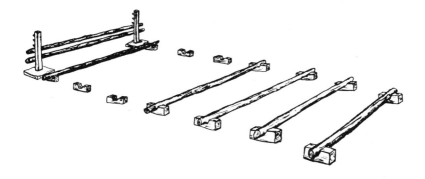

The instructor can go one step further if he considers it desirable, removing bar 4 and increasing the height of the jump to three feet. Here again, the deciding factor will be the capabilities and experience of his pupils and of their horses.

Obviously, the procedure to be followed in using cavalletti as described above is basically very simple. However, to use it effectively, the instructor should have clearly in mind what he is seeking to accomplish by this method of starting jump instruction. Used properly, the jump at the end of the grid ceases to be a separate obstacle and becomes merely a continuation of the grid. The pupil has no problem of rating his horse. The horse is automatically placed at the right spot to make a little hop, first over a very low jump, and then progressively over slightly higher jumps. The pupil takes a jumping position on entering the grid and quietly maintains that position through the grid and over the jump at the end. The intent is to remove entirely any tendency of the pupil to brace and tighten as the jump approaches. Initially, it is generally advisable for the rider to use a posting trot, but when the rhythm is well established and as soon as the rider can do so without loss of stability or interference with the horse, a sitting trot should be substituted. With some riders and some horses it may be difficult to obtain a smooth, balanced ride while sitting, and in such cases it is proper to continue working at the posting trot. Every effort should be made to secure a quiet ride through the grid on a loose rein, but never at the risk of permitting the horse to break into a canter going through the grid. If the horse starts to canter, the rider should, if possible, turn him off to the side and not let him continue through the grid. If the rider has continuing difficulty in holding the horse to a trot, he should go back to the previous stage, for example, removing the jump at the end of the grid if one is being used, or returning to a walk if the plain grid is being used with no jump at the end.

With all this in mind, a few further words of warning. Again, we must emphasize: do not hurry. If all you are able to accomplish in your first lesson is a calm, quiet walk over the cavalletti, this is adequate. Only a part of each period should be devoted to cavalletti. If it takes a week of instruction to have all your pupils trotting boldly but quietly over the grid, don't be concerned. Don't accept anything less than a completely calm and relaxed ride, both from the pupil and the horse. Initially, the jump at the end of the grid should be the lowest height which will cause the horse to jump. We have indicated that cavalletti is very flexible and can be varied in many different ways. This is also true of the specific method just described. For example, it cannot be said that there is anything sacred about starting with seven poles for a grid rather than five, six, eight, or nine. However, unless you are absolutely sure you know precisely what you are seeking to accomplish, you will be wise to adhere to the method and program outlined. I have seen the value of cavalletti almost completely lost because of the instructor's failure to adhere to the sound basic principles described above.

Let us suppose that your instruction has gone well. Your pupils are relaxed and sitting well with a secure seat and their horses are moving relaxed and calmly. What can we do next? A very simple device is to ask each pupil to close his eyes as he enters the grid and to ride through the grid and over the jump with his eyes closed. Obviously, the rider can accomplish this successfully only if he is maintaining a proper jumping position. Another excellent variation is to have each rider drop the reins as he enters the grid and ride through without the reins. If all goes well, the rider can then extend his arms to each side and ride through with his arms outstretched.

We can also extend the use of the cavalletti by adding a second low jump, giving us an in and out. The distance will depend on the size and boldness of the horses used, but as a start try 18 feet. If the horses are big and bold, the distance can be increased, but bear in mind that what we are aiming for at this point is a quiet, relaxed performance, and neither in height nor in distance between jumps should the obstacle be at all demanding. In due course, additional jumps may be added up to a total of five or six jumps. Also, the character of the jumps may be varied, so although we are still using little jumps, we can use in miniature a great variety of obstacles, for example, oxers, hogs backs, double or triple bars, etc.

All having gone well up to this point, we can now eliminate the grid altogether, returning only to a single low jump placed at a suitable distance in front of our second and major obstacle. Since our low jump is now being used for the purpose of placing our horse in his approach to the major jump, I will now refer to this not as cavalletti but as the placing jump. It should still be low; 18 inches is plenty. Initially, the jump itself should be of modest height, not over 2-1/2 or possibly three feet. The spacing jump will be jumped at the trot, so the distance from the spacing jump to the jump should be moderate, say 17 to 20 feet, depending on the size and scope of the horse. As the schooling progresses, the jump may be increased in height up to the capacity of the horse and rider, with the spacing jump, however, still remaining not over 18 inches. The distance to the main jump will, however, increase as the jump is raised in height.

Before asking for any substantial increase in the height of the jump, it will generally be found more useful to make constant changes in the type of jump. Modest or even miniature triple bars, hogs backs, oxers, walls, and indeed any type of jump which the horse may later encounter in more substantial size should be used at this stage. The whole effort is to secure a quiet, relaxed performance with the horse taking off at precisely the desired distance in front of the jump. Do not forget that to achieve this perfect takeoff, it may be necessary to adjust the distance between the spacing jump and the jump.

Do not hurry your work. If any sign of excitement appears, return to working over the grid, or even to a plain grid without any raised obstacle at the end. Indeed, even if everything is going well, an occasional return to work over the grid will be found helpful. But let us assume that at the end of two or three days' or two or three weeks' work, or whatever longer time is indicated, you are quite satisfied with the performance achieved in taking the placement jump at the trot.

Now you can permit the horse to take the placing jump at the canter. For this, you will increase the distance from the placing jump to the jump. Again, the exact distance will depend on size and scope, but for most horses the correct distance will be found to be in the range of 20 to 24 feet.

Another use of the "little jump" which is not ordinarily thought of as part of cavalletti but which is perhaps worth mentioning as a useful training device is the placing of the small jump beyond the main jump. The purpose is to cause the horse to collect himself, drop his head, and observe his footing and the spacing of his stride after taking the jump. A normal distance would be 22 to 24 feet beyond the main jump. However, this distance can be shortened (as a device for training the horse to collect himself and come quickly in hand after landing) or lengthened (if it is desired to have the horse extend his stride and move out boldly upon landing). These, however, are techniques of training to be used with discretion by an experienced instructor working with competent riders on adequate horses.

The description of cavalletti as so far presented has been directed to certain very specific applications which are believed to be especially adaptable for general use by Pony Club instructors. Cavalletti can be used in other ways, and to round out the picture, we now present a description of two such uses.

The first is the use of cavalletti as a piece of equipment or as building blocks for constructing jumps of various types and sizes. This use of cavalletti is well described in *The Pony Club Instructors Handbook* on pages 53–55, and in *The Manual of Horsemanship* on pages 28–30. This type of cavalletti provides in a flexible and inexpensive form a variety in jump construction which might not otherwise be available. However, the end result is merely an obstacle to be jumped like any other jump, and there is no special technique applicable to jumping obstacles so constructed.

Now we come to the use of cavalletti as a series of

obstacles to be jumped at the canter. This use is very well described in the British Pony Club film entitled "Training Over Cavalletti and Grid," a 20-minute sound film which is available for rental from the film library of the U.S.P.C. In its simplest form, the grid will be made up of a series of five or more jumps spaced so that there will be one canter stride between jumps. Exact spacing, as always, will depend on the height of the cavalletti and the size and scope of the horses used. For the average horse, a distance of 20 feet will ordinarily be appropriate. The next basic form of grid is composed of jumps placed so that the horse lands and immediately takes off over the next jump. For this, a spacing of about 11 feet will be appropriate for the average horse. Now we can vary our grid by placing some jumps 20 feet apart, some 11 feet apart, and we can also extend the spacing to approximately 30 feet so that two canter strides will be taken between jumps. The basic grid is ordinarily constructed of single-pole obstacles all of the same type and initially, at least, not over 18 inches in height. But now we can introduce a wide variety of obstacles; all, however, must be within the height range at which we are working. For extended jumps, parallel bars, a triple bar, a hogs back, or a chicken coop are obvious possibilities. For upright jumps, any kind of fence, simulated stone wall, or other solid-appearing obstacle can be used. If the work has been going well, at least some of the jumps can be increased in height. The ingenuity of the course builder and the availability of material are the only limitations. The course builder should obviously keep in mind the basic principle of more or less alternating extended and upright obstacles. A grid permanently constructed of solid, immovable objects (for example, heavy logs fastened on top of short posts) has the obvious advantage that the jumps cannot be knocked down or displaced, and the very solidity of the jumps encourages good, careful jumping. However, such a course is lacking in flexibility and is recommended only if there is also other movable material available from which more varied courses can be constructed and changed from time to time as may be desired. In England, at one time at least, grids were constructed with wings or side walls so that once started through the grid, the horse could not run out. This type of grid was then jumped without reins or without stirrups. The grid in this form has rarely been used in the U.S.A.

And now one final warning. The methods suggested will greatly facilitate the introduction of the pupil to jumping and, properly used, should greatly help the pupil to stay with his horse, to remain supple and relaxed, and to avoid being left behind. But it is still true that great discretion should be used by the instructor in selecting those pupils who are to receive even elementary jumping instruction. The basic principle should still be that the pupil must achieve a firm seat and at least reasonably good hands before any attempt at jumping should be permitted.

Chapter VII

The Development of the Ordinary and Strong Gaits, Paces, and Figures on a Single-Track

The rider can develop a springy regular, ordinary, and strong walk, and trot and canter through the use of his driving aids while maintaining the correct sequence of the gaits. Then, by guiding the horse accurately through the figures, a horse is able to go on a single-track. The rider should influence his horse mainly with his legs and weight, and as little as possible with his hands. No force should be used to make a horse flexible and supple. Again, long rides outdoors, preferably over light, hilly terrain and low jumps (mostly from the trot) will strengthen the horse's muscles and will make his joints more flexible. All riders are inclined to use their hands too much. Inadvertently, they do not allow the horse to move freely and in a relaxed way from the rear to the front. If a horse cannot relax the back muscles, he cannot find his balance.

No horse is able to respond to the diagonal aids at the beginning. Only one-sided aids can be used to make the horse respond. For this reason, the instructor and rider should start on a big circle. In order to balance himself, a horse will accept the rider's driving inside leg by bending his body around the rider's leg. The rider should move his outside hand forward *(relax the tension on the outside rein).* This will make the horse yield to the inside hand. By changing from one circle to the other all horses respond willingly, so that the rider can gradually bring his horse to accept his inside leg and outside rein. The rider no longer needs to go forward with his outside hand. Gradually, the rider will be able to use both legs and both hands to make the horse yield, and the horse will relax and move freely forward. The rider must be able to establish this free forward movement in the ordinary and strong paces progressively. Horses who show resistance should not be punished or disciplined. Only work on the circle will make it possible for the horse to find his own balance and to move forward in a relaxed manner.

After the horse goes willingly forward and is light on the bit, the rider can guide his horse in smaller circles and serpentines. All horses will gradually be able to bend their spine, ribs, and neck. Every horse will drop his head and neck on his own so that the rider, by the use of his driving aids, can keep a light and steady contact between his hands and the horse's mouth. The rider should never try to achieve this by seesawing or by pulling backward with his hands.

Once the rider has patiently established this contact with his driving aids, the horse will show no resistance to the rider's legs or hands. No rider has to use sliding reins or chambons. The latter are, in my opinion, neckbreakers. Both types of reins hinder the horse's ability to move freely forward and also interfere with the proper sequence in all paces. They also prevent the horse from bending his hip joint.

Another great help in achieving a response from the horse is bending left or right in the full stop. The rider must first have his horse standing evenly on all four legs. By moving forward with the left or right hand, every horse will yield to the pressure of the bit on the opposite side. Every horse will also respond the same way while in motion. The rider should practice this often. When a horse responds willingly, the rider can then ask his horse to bend only in the poll. He must first wait until the horse is light on both reins. If the rider then takes one hand a little higher and uses the opposite restraining rein, the horse will keep his neck straight and will bend his head only slightly to that side. These exercises are very helpful for the rider in achieving a correct bending of the horse's head and neck. If a horse shows a tendency to step sideward in the opposite direction with his hind legs, the rider must either use his leg on that side or make effective use of a fence or wall. All of this is much easier for horse and rider in motion.

When a horse responds to all the important aids mentioned, the rider should start to train his horse to be attentive to his aids. *The rider has the half-halt to help him achieve this.* The earlier the rider learns how to coordinate his aids, the earlier he will be able to train his horse. The horse should move freely on the rider's driving aids, with regularity of movement in the proper sequence of the gaits. There should be light contact between the rider's hands and the horse's mouth. The rider should only feel the weight of the reins in his hands. A well-balanced horse is able to move in this manner. The instructor and rider have to realize that the rider's weight will consistently bring the horse on the forehand. For this reason the half-halts are of great importance to combat this tendency and to maintain the necessary light contact. In time, the horse will quickly respond to the half-halts if the rider uses only his braced back and a turn of his wrist, and the horse will move briskly forward in a balanced and relaxed manner. Also, in a short time the horse will feel the aids and respond if the rider simply braces his back and closes his hands as though squeezing a sponge. The half-halts have to be given frequently to keep a horse balanced, relaxed, and attentive. Riders have to learn to coordinate their aids in sequence as explained. *The strength of these aids depends entirely on each horse's responsiveness and sensitivity.* A well-trained horse can then perform—step-by-step and stride-by-stride—on the rider's driving aids with very light contact on the reins. A horse must be trained to walk, trot, canter, and respond to the half-halts. Only then is it possible for the horse to stay relaxed and balanced.

Horses that are losing their balance will either resist the rider's aids or will lean on the rider's hands. They will tighten their back muscles and use their hind legs to resist the rider's hands. By working the horse in figures, such as circles, figure eights, or serpentines, the rider will be able to influence the horse to yield to his hands and become light on his hands by pushing the horse's inside hind leg forward with his inside leg, and by bending the horse's neck to the inside. The horse will then become balanced by relaxing his back muscles again and using both hind legs to move freely forward. The rider can then squeeze both legs, brace his back, and fix both hands.

The rider must keep in mind that his leg aids can only drive a horse forward or sideward. His hands can only be fixed or relaxed and his back, by being braced, has to assist his legs or his hands. In all gaits, paces, or figures the rider's aids are the same. The horse has to respond and accept these aids lightly and willingly.

The rider can also ask the horse to respond while riding with only one hand. This proves that the horse is responsive and sensitive. Taking the reins in one hand in the early stage of training gives the rider the assurance that they are progressing in the right direction. The reins should be in the left hand or the right hand, so that the left rein is inside from left to right, and the right rein is inside from right to left in the rider's hand. A turn of the wrist to the left or right should be enough of a motion if the rider has to make the horse yield to the hand. To get the horse and rider accustomed to it, this should be done first in the full stop, then in the walk. Later the rider will be able to do it also in the trot and canter, especially while riding cross-country. The free right or left hand should be carried behind the rider's thigh.

In the beginning of training, it is advisable to practice riding with one hand only at the end of the practice session and only at the walk. The momentum is then slow and the rider has ample time to coordinate his aids. When this is patiently done, the horse will respond quickly and will make the further development of horse and rider more enjoyable.

Self-discipline of the rider is of utmost importance from the very beginning of the training of the horse. The rider must realize that he has to strengthen the horse's muscles and guide the horse, with the influence of his aids, through exercises which make the horse's body flexible. This is the unwritten law under which every horse has to work, regardless of the purpose for which the rider wants to use him.

Another helpful exercise for making the horse responsive is to ride him on a straight line in left or right position. This is achieved by bending the horse's neck to the left or right, with the rider's inside leg urging the horse's inside hind leg to step between the front legs. The outside leg of the rider must urge the outside hind

Ordinary trot with reins in one hand (Saddlebred).

Position right (Thoroughbred).

leg of the horse in the direction of the outside front leg. This exercise is very helpful in keeping the horse well-balanced and light on the bit. Also, in turning figures, the rider can guide his horse in the left or right position not only by bending the horse to the inside but also to the outside. This can be done in all three gaits and will improve the balance of every horse. Riding in position is also a simple preparation for the horse and rider for all two-track exercises, especially if the rider effectively urges his horse to step with his inside or outside hind leg between the front legs.

The rider should now introduce his horse slowly to all fundamental figures for the development of the horse's flexibility. To be able to guide his horse with

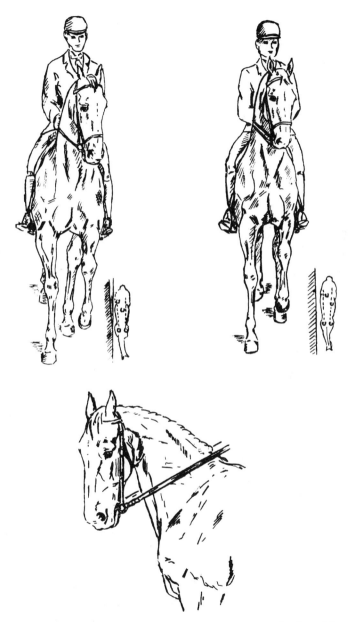

Position left. Left hind leg and alternately right hind leg stepping between the front legs and bending the neck in the poll only.

his seat, the rider must practice leg-yielding, the turn on the forelegs, and the turn on the haunches. Also to be practiced are the transitions from ordinary to strong paces, transitions from one gait to the other, the full stop, and backing. This is time-consuming and should be done patiently and gradually. The purpose is to improve the horse's longitudinal and lateral flexibility.

It is advisable to start with the turn on the forelegs. Every horse will accept the right rein and right leg quickly and turn to the left with his hindquarters. The rider should execute this exercise slowly and lead the horse step by step around the horse's inside front leg. It must be emphasized that the "inside" is the side to which a horse is bent. If the horse steps forward, the rider should immediately execute a half-halt. Stepping forward is a lesser fault than stepping backward. When a horse steps backward this indicates too strong an influence of the rider's hands. The turn on the forehand should be done from the full stop and practiced in both directions. By executing this figure, the rider learns to use his legs properly and to coordinate his aids. The horse will be trained to bend his spine, ribs, and neck by becoming sensitive and responsive to the rider's aids. The horse will also become more flexible in his hip and shoulder joints. Most horses have difficulty bending their right hip joint sideward. This is the reason one sees many horses tilting their heads to the left and lowering their right ears. This is a result of the horse's not being flexible longitudinally and laterally. The contact from the rider's left hand becomes so strong that the horse, because of the pressure on the left side of his mouth, brings his mouth to the left, thus tilting his head to the left and causing the lowering of his right ear. The rider can overcome difficulties by using the right rein more to assist the right leg, or vice versa. In the beginning, the rider must be satisfied with one or two steps. He should pet his horse often if the horse responds and yields to his leg aids.

The rider should not attempt to execute the turn on the haunches until the horse responds to leg-yielding with the outside leg. The rider must use his leg so that the horse yields to the pressure and moves his hind legs away from the track. The front legs move on the track, the hind legs move at a 45-degree angle to the track in a forward-sideward motion. In the beginning, the rider can also use the outside rein more to assist his leg so that the horse yields to the outside leg. The rider should first ask for one or two steps before the horse can willingly and regularly yield to the rider's left or right leg. The rider should train the horse to bend his whole body from poll to tail and to flex the hip and shoulder joints not only up and down but also sideward. For the rider, it is very important to learn to coordinate his aids, and most important to strengthen and to use his legs properly. The rider must constantly be certain that his upper body remains straight. By holding his shoulders back, the rider will be able to ride the horse at a brisk and regular pace forward and sideward. These exercises improve the horse laterally. *The rider can now influence the horse with his forward and sideward driving aids.* In a short time, the horse will be able to yield to the rider's leg while going correctly through the corners.

When half-halts are used by the rider, step-by-step in the corners, every horse can make a turn on the haunches without losing impulsion. The transition from one gait to the other and to the full stop will make every horse flexible enough so that the rider can ask for the turn on the haunches from the full stop. It is important that the exact four-beat sequence of the walk is not lost.

The flexibility of the horse's body at this point will enable the rider to back the horse. By squeezing both legs and bracing his back, the rider can make the horse go forward if he relaxes his hands. By keeping his hands fixed, he can make the horse step back. The rider has to be satisfied if the horse steps back only one step at first. Petting the horse and repeating this command will train the horse to go backward for as many steps as the rider asks.

The rider can now expect the horse to move forward by lengthening his steps and strides in the same rhythm as in the ordinary gaits. The horse will lengthen his base of support as long as the rider is able to keep him relaxed and balanced. This is only possible if the rider pays attention to the horse's relaxation. Every horse who is pushed too much by his rider will lose his balance. In order to keep himself balanced, the horse will lean more on the rider's hands by tightening his back muscles. In time, the horse will go forward, but will do so in faster, exaggerated steps and will be tense. The rider should avoid this under all circumstances. Undue hardship in the further development of horse and rider can thus be avoided.

To lengthen his steps and strides, every horse first has to use his back muscles. He is then able to use more thrust with his hind legs and is able to bend his hip joint, using it more like a spring. A very great help to improve the forward thrust of the hind legs is jumping—free or with the rider. Cavalletti work and more up- and downhill rides outdoors will make a horse more flexible longitudinally and therefore able to stay relaxed and to lengthen his base of support. In this way, every horse can be trained to lengthen his steps and strides. The horse then can move relaxed, balanced, and in the same rhythm and impulsion, harmoniously forward in the strong gaits.

The horse can develop and achieve the ordinary canter on the outside leg by going in a big circle, preferably outdoors. The rider should strike off into the canter after changing from the inside leg to the outside

leg by bringing the horse to the walk. Every horse will
not be able to do this in the beginning, and will trot.
The rider should patiently use half-halts during the
transition until the horse walks, and then should strike
off into the canter on the opposite leg. By repeating
this command patiently and often, every horse will become more flexible and will walk. When the rider has
been able to make his horse respond with the walk, he
will find it very easy for the horse to accept his aids.
The rider must alert the horse for the next command by
using half-halts so that his horse is attentive. As soon
as the rider feels that the horse is attentive, he is able to
bring the horse to the walk when the horse has reached
the second beat of the canter, when the horse already
has three of his legs on the ground. This makes it possible for the horse to walk immediately. In the beginning, the rider does not have to pay attention to the
number of steps his horse walks. It is important that
the horse accept the rider's aids and remain calm and
relaxed. Should the horse become nervous and not
walk in a relaxed manner, the rider can successfully
use leg-yielding with either the left or right leg to calm
the horse. In time, the rider should be able to strike off
into the canter after three steps in the walk. This is possible if the rider has been patiently training the horse
so that he can use "riding in position" in the ordinary
gaits or "shoulder-fore" in the collected gaits successfully to either side.

These simple changes of leg improve the horse longitudinally and make it easy for the rider to ride the
counterlead in the enclosed arena. The rider should
practice often in the ring and, when the horse is accustomed to it, for long periods of time. The counterlead
then improves the horse's longitudinal and lateral
flexibility. The rider will feel that he can drive the
horse increasingly more forward. By frequently using
half-halts, especially in the corners, the rider can be as-

sured that the horse will find his balance. If the rider feels the horse staying relaxed and balanced, he can improve the horse's flexibility by guiding him in the counterlead on a circle or in serpentines.

The rider can and should convince himself that the horse canters relaxed and balanced by moving his hands forward. The best timing for this is when the rider's hips advance forward in the saddle. He should straighten his arms, moving his hands forward and above the manecomb. When a horse keeps his head and neck carriage for the few seconds during which the rider moves his hands forward and back, the rider can be assured of the horse's balance. The rider should also move his hands forward in both the walk and trot. By increasing and decreasing the countercanter, figures such as circles, figure eights, serpentines, and even transitions can improve every horse not only longitudinally but also laterally. After a short time the rider will be able to feel that the horse can balance himself. The horse will flex his hip joint more by bringing his inside hind leg further forward in order to keep his balance. The rider can also feel that the horse is bending his spine and ribs around the rider's inside leg smoothly and easily. He will also feel that the horse will canter perfectly straight (on one track) by using the outside rein pressed against the neck. Should the horse lean more on one rein than the other, the rider can correct this by bending the horse to that side. This shoulder-fore position can be used by the rider in all gaits and paces. *In this way the horse will give the rider the correct collected gaits.*

The rider will find that all horses become very flexible in all gaits and figures in this stage of training. Combined with alternately riding cross-country and over jumps in ordinary and strong gaits, every horse can be brought to perfection in these fundamental requirements; that is, complete relaxation and balance in all gaits and paces, with regular steps and strides. This is an accepted fact, regardless of the rider's ambition, and is necessary for the improvement of all horses. For the future Grand Prix horse it is a *must.*

Regardless of the rider's ambition and the horse's ability, the rider should be able to shorten or to lengthen the horse's base of support. The horse is now able to use his muscles properly and can flex his joints for the benefit of the rider and himself. The rider can and should incorporate all of the exercises described in his daily work and while he is warming up the horse, regardless of which equestrian discipline he starts. Because of the high standard required in International and Olympic competition, the horse and rider have to go through a very specialized training program. Horses with great jumping ability have to be schooled over higher jumps and more difficult combinations. Horses with great stamina and boldness have to be schooled over difficult terrain and a variety of jumps. The training of the dressage horse must conform to the prescribed exercises.

Chapter VIII

Stage II–Exercises to Develop the Horse's Longitudinal and Lateral Flexibility

It cannot be stressed too often that the rider must work with the horse's way of moving; that is, from the rear to the front, so that the horse will perform certain figures in the gaits in a relaxed and balanced manner. If the rider works against the horse's nature, it will be impossible for the horse to be obedient. The rider must pay attention to his driving seat so that he is able to feel the horse's muscles and be sensitive to the horse's movements and responses.

The rider who studies the skeletal system of the horse will find that there is a limit to the amount that a horse can bend his body evenly from poll to tail. He should bear this in mind in all of his work sessions. The rider should also think about the way in which the horse can best use his hind legs to maintain regular forward impulsion: he must develop the horse, through exercises, to find the cadence needed to correctly perform the collected and extended gaits; he has to exercise the horse in figures which will develop the horse's hind legs so that he can carry more of his and the rider's weight; he must use his driving seat to develop the power of the horse's hind legs to carry horse and rider forward. The rider who painstakingly pays strict attention to practicing the correct exercises to develop the horse's flexibility and suppleness will not have difficulty in developing the power of the horse's hind legs, which must step in the footprints of the front legs.

The carefully developed horse has acquired strong muscles and supple joints, as well as a supple back, so that he can bend his spine and ribs to the left and to the right from poll to tail. As a result of the exercises described so far in this book, the horse should now be obedient to the rider's aids, and the rider can begin to develop his horse longitudinally as well as laterally. The horse is now well prepared for the collected and extended gaits and paces. These gaits and paces have to be very lively, with impulsion and cadence. The transitions from ordinary to strong gaits and paces, and vice versa, as well as the transition to the full stop and backing (one or two horse lengths) help the rider to improve the horse's longitudinal flexibility. The shoulder-in, haunches-in, and haunches-out figures help to improve the horse's lateral flexibility. *It is of utmost importance that the rider keep the horse's hind legs very active so that the horse will lower his croup by bending his hip joint.* If that is accomplished, and the rider has paid attention to the fact that the horse is relaxed, the horse will sooner or later increase the up-and-down movement of his front and hind legs. *This is a reflex motion of the horse's extensor and flexor muscles, and is called cadence.* A horse must perform the collected and extended gaits and all movements on two-tracks with impulsion and cadence in the same rhythm.

It will be very difficult for rider and horse to perform exercises and figures correctly if the horse is not re-laxed and balanced at all times. A horse which is not relaxed, and balanced will resist the rider's aids, and the rider will then be unable to perform with invisible aids. This in turn will make it difficult for the rider and horse to perform effectively, especially at the Grand Prix level. Because of the resistance of the horse, caused by the horse's stiffness and lack of balance, the rider will be forced to drill his horse instead of training the horse to perform. Drilling is always evident when the horse shortens his neck and goes too strongly against the rider's hands. It is also evidenced by the lack of correct bending to the right or left (bending to the left is usually the most difficult), and by exaggerat-ed stretching of the legs—all of which is very visible. This might impress the layman, but to the trained eye of the expert it denotes tension. Horses which perform in tension might be able to perform the figures, but the creative art of riding is lost. The horse loses his grace-ful and harmonious way of moving. *Only if the rider maintains the relaxation and the balance of the horse can he, as well as the horse, perform correct tests.*

It takes considerable time to train a horse and make him responsive to the rider's aids. It also takes a rider considerable time and hard work to develop strength in his own body so that he will be physically capable of giving strong aids to the horse so that the horse can perform the required exercises.

Shoulder-in and haunches-in and -out, as well as traversals and increasing and decreasing gaits, will bring the success necessary for all the F.E.I. tests. In all the two-track movements a horse has to be bent evenly from poll to tail. The rider has to bend the horse around his inside leg. To achieve this, and also to train the horse to lower his croup by maintaining his forward impulsion and cadence, the rider starts with shoulder-in and with increasing and decreasing the trot. A horse which is prepared for this by leg-yielding exercises with both the inside and outside leg will have no difficulty in performing these other exercises. Because of his obedience to the rider's leg aids, the horse will be able to bend his hip joint in such a way that he can move his stifle sideward as well as up and down. This flexibility is necessary for the horse to move with ease and harmony forward and sideward. It is of great importance for the rider to use both legs to animate the horse's hind legs, although it is the rider's outside leg which bends the horse's spine and ribs around his inside leg. Because of the use of leg aids in all exercises and figures, the rider does not use his hands to influence the horse's movements in two-track exercises. The rider will feel that the horse's inside back and neck muscles will contract and the outside back and neck muscles will extend. Frequent half-halts will keep the horse relaxed and balanced so that the horse can go forward-sideward with regular steps and strides. It is easiest for the horse and rider to achieve this in the walk. When this is accomplished, the rider should practice these exercises at the trot and canter as well. It is very important that the horse be light on the bit. To maintain his forward impulsion, the horse's inside hind leg must follow his outside front leg. When the horse willingly goes shoulder-in at the walk, trot, and canter, the rider can practice haunches-in and haunches-out. The rider should do this first in the walk in the same way as described for the shoulder-in exercise, but in such a way that the outside hind leg follows the inside front leg. To reiterate, the side of the horse which is bent around the rider's leg is called the inside.

It is not difficult to develop the traversals in the

The Shoulder-in.

The Haunches-in.

walk, trot, and canter from the preceding three exercises. In the beginning the rider should ride haunches-in on the crossing line and, after the horse is accustomed to this, allow the horse to go parallel to the wall. During all these exercises the rider will be able to feel the horse's back become more and more relaxed. The horse, being light on the bit, will move regularly forward and sideward in complete balance. To be certain that the horse always leads with his shoulders aligned slightly ahead of his hindquarters, the rider should first ride shoulder-in and then perform the traversal. The rider should also ride shoulder-in for one or two steps and strides before changing direction. In this way the horse will become accustomed to bending his spine and ribs correctly before going in the opposite direction. The rider is able to feel that his horse will stay on his inside leg and outside rein in all two-track figures. A rider who pays attention to the proper bend of the horse's body will find that the horse will also bend his spine and ribs in the flying changes.

Before the rider can ask the horse to execute the flying change, he has to ride many transitions from the collected canter to the collected walk. The horse has to canter on every time in the opposite lead, preferably while executing a figure eight or a serpentine. After this simple change of lead can be executed very smoothly and effortlessly, the rider should ask the horse to execute the flying change.

In the beginning, the flying change can be executed more readily from the counter lead at the corners of the exercise ring. Some horses find it easier to execute the flying change when changing from one circle to another; other horses find it easier to execute the flying change in serpentines when crossing the middle line. A rider has to discover which way his horse responds to the aids. It is necessary for the rider to first give strong and distinct aids with his legs, but he must be

Mrs. Kaethe Franke on *Bojar,* performing two-tracking.

able to relax so that the horse learns to change leads (or execute flying changes) with the slightest pressure from the rider's legs—more specifically, from his calves. The rider has to bear in mind that the horse can make the flying change only when all four legs are in the air—during the suspension of the horse. This is the moment when the rider's hips move forward in the saddle. In this split second the rider must give the signal with his legs to urge the horse to change leads (or execute the flying change). The rider who trains his horse to be obedient to his leg aids through leg-yielding exercises can, without bringing the horse on two-tracks, use the same aids to obtain response from the horse to make the flying change. In a very short period of time the rider will feel that the horse will bend his spine and ribs to the left or right in response to pressure from the opposite leg. It should be mentioned here that a rider cannot avoid the horse's being nervous when first asked to execute the flying change. If the horse becomes excited when asked to perform this figure or if he doesn't execute this figure properly, the rider must avoid any action which will make the horse more excited. Patience on the rider's part will prove to be very beneficial and will achieve the best results. A rider must be patient and gently persuasive, and never punish the horse if, at first, the flying changes are not correct. The horse should be brought to a walk immediately if the flying change is improperly executed, and brought back on the aids. Then, when the rider feels that the horse is relaxed and balanced, he can ask for the flying change again. With an easily excited horse, or with a very sensitive horse, it may take longer than usual. When the horse accepts the rider's aids, the rider can then ask the horse to execute the flying change often so that the horse will perform this figure in a relaxed manner, showing no excitement or stiffness. Riding without spurs will help to keep the horse calm and relaxed. The greatest fault of the rider is to try to help the horse with his upper body. The rider must sit very firmly in the saddle. He must keep his shoulders back, his knees down, and he must especially keep his hands very steady. Only in this way will the rider be prepared to give a half-halt if the horse quickens his pace when he is given the signal for a flying change.

If the horse stays relaxed on the rider's aids, the rider will be able to feel, during the suspension, that the horse, while keeping his balance, contracts his back muscles to the right or left. The horse also contracts his neck muscles. The rider will feel the horse bend his spine evenly from poll to tail, on his own effort. After the rider has established this, he should frequently cross the ring in the extended canter, and while he decreases the gait to the collected canter and the horse accepts the half-halts and is light on the bit, he can make certain that the horse uses his hind legs and shoulders freely so it becomes visible that the horse is "flying forward" to change the lead.

In this stage the rider should start to get a higher degree of collection by allowing his horse to walk in half steps forward more frequently. The rider thus trains his horse to accept the strong driving aids while staying light on the bit. The horse will respond to the rider's aids by keeping his back relaxed, and will then step forward in half steps in cadence. This is only possible for the horse when he bends his hip joints. At the same time the horse, being used to the half-halt, will yield to the rider's hands and erect himself. After a few steps this must be changed to a vigorous extended trot or canter and repeated many times until the horse can stay relaxed and calm on the rider's aids. This exercise is very important to prepare the horse for the piaffe, passage, pirouette, and flying change on a certain number of strides.

All horses worked in exercises on two-tracks must keep both ears at the same height. Horses who tilt their heads are either being forced to execute a figure or not being properly guided. Lack of flexibility in the right hip joint will cause the horse to lower the right ear, and vice versa. Only leg-yielding can correct this problem by making the horse more flexible laterally.

By performing all the exercises described in this chapter, the rider will be able to bring the horse to such a stage of flexibility and sensitivity that he will be in a position to maintain a good driving seat and to give invisible aids. Only stiffness in the horse's body can force the rider to do otherwise. *A rider has to bear in mind that he is not the teacher of the horse, but that through his understanding and feeling he trains and makes it possible for the horse to perform the tests issued by the F.E.I. and used in International and Olympic events with ease, grace, impulsion and cadence—and in beauty and harmony.* A rider who wants to compete against selected riders from other countries has to bear in mind that his horse must have a flexible body. *Only a rider who strengthens the horse's muscles and makes his horse's joints and spine flexible will be successful.* A finished, trained Grand Prix horse needs to practice all the prescribed exercises in his daily training to stay supple and flexible and remain on the rider's aids. Therefore, a rider who thinks that a trained horse performs by himself will sooner or later find that this is not so. The rider has to learn how to influence the horse with his aids through his seat. Only a rider with a strong driving seat will be able to bring his horse to a higher degree of collection, especially while decreasing the gaits. Decreasing the gaits of a horse is not slowing the horse down with the hands alone. Because of the greater momentum a horse has in the extended gaits, it is not as easy to decrease the gait as some riders think. Here, too, the rider has to give half-halts as explained before. To accomplish this, the rider's legs, braced back, and fixed hands have to be strong. Every rider can use leg-yielding very effectively during the transition to achieve the desired results. A properly trained horse will respond easily to all commands, even when the rider holds all of the reins in one hand.

Chapter IX

The Development of the Collected and Extended Gaits and Figures on Single- and Two-Tracks

Before describing the further development of the horse's gaits and figures, it should be mentioned that, as in all equestrian disciplines, the rider who has decided to compete in International competition has to have a suitable horse. This means that the horse is well balanced and sensitive by nature, and is thus worth training to the Grand Prix level. This type of horse makes training enjoyable as well as worthwhile. *The horse must have good gaits with visible shoulder freedom and good thrust with the hind legs. The horse also needs a good, strong back, good withers, and a long neck which is not set on the shoulder too high or too low.*

The gymnastic training of the horse is of utmost importance for the horse's achievement of a higher degree of suppleness, flexibility, and collection. This can be achieved by the rider who pays strict attention to his driving seat. He must realize that the more he wants to collect the horse, the more strongly he has to influence the horse with the driving aids. The collection must come from the horse's hindquarters. The joints have to be made more flexible so that the horse can bend them more and therefore lowers his croup. By lowering the croup, the horse uses the extensor and flexor muscles more, and thus is able to perform all of the collected and extended gaits with great impulsion and in cadence. The flexibility and the ability to carry more weight with the hindquarters will enable the horse to execute all two-track movements, culminating in the counterchanges in the trot and canter. This training goes beyond the requirements of the Pony Clubs.

By continuous practice of the appropriate exercises and figures described in this book, the horse will attain the flexibility and suppleness necessary to develop the collected and extended gaits. This flexibility and suppleness can also be achieved by riding frequently on the bridlepath.

It is equally important for the rider to remember that no matter how hard he works, he will be successful (especially in International competition) only if he works in harmony with the horse's nature. This development of the horse's body through practicing correct exercises and figures in proper sequence will improve the horse's flexibility and suppleness as well as develop the horse progressively.

A rider who trains the horse in this method daily, and does not forget to alternate brisk and vigorous impulsion in all gaits and paces, will form the foundation for the horse to perform in harmonious and cadenced collected and extended gaits. The rider now has to pay the utmost attention to his driving seat since without this the horse is not able to maintain impulsion and cadence.

Further, the rider who has trained the horse in the

prescribed method will feel the horse's willingness to accept the rider's driving aids in the counterlead. The rider can use this to his advantage to bring the horse from ordinary to collected paces without shortening the horse's neck and, consequently, without disturbing the horse's steps and strides. The horse is able to maintain the correct sequence of his gaits. Slowly but surely, the rider is in the position to be able to make many transitions through which the horse, by his own effort, develops the collected and extended paces.

To maintain and strengthen the achieved stage in the training period, the rider should frequently ride outdoors on the bridlepath and limber up his horse with the exercises in the ordinary and strong gaits until he can drive his horse forward. Only then should the rider ask his horse to perform the exercises in the collected and extended gaits. If there is no time to ride outdoors, the rider should longe the horse. *The rider must always keep in mind that the collected and extended paces are fatiguing for the horse's muscles, and can thus impair the flexibility of the joints.*

The rider should develop all paces and figures in collection from the correct shoulder-fore, or shoulder-in, position. Only this will give the rider the assurance and the feeling that the horse is using the inside hind leg. Without it, no horse is able to maintain impulsion, balance, and the correct bending of his body.

The horse can be trained to perform shoulder-in correctly by the use of leg-yielding with the rider's inside leg. The rider has only to press his inside leg against the horse so that the horse's inside hind leg will follow the outside front leg. The horse will follow the outside front leg. The horse will then bring his shoulder in, so that he moves on two-tracks at a 30 to 35 degree angle, instead of the 45 degree angle used in leg-yielding. In this way the horse will not, and cannot, cross his legs. Only then is the rider able to maintain the impulsion through his driving seat, and only by giving half-halts is the rider able to develop and keep the cadence necessary for all collected and extended gaits. *Shoulder-in is used for all collected and extended paces, and all the figures in high collection on single- or on two-tracks. Leg-yielding is used to develop the ordinary and strong paces and all figures on a single-track.*

Once a rider has established the collected and extended paces and the shoulder-in, it is not difficult to guide the horse to bring his haunches in or out, or to go on the crossing line using the haunches-in. When the horse can go parallel to the wall, the latter is a traversal or half-pass (or as it is called in the F.E.I. tests, a two-track). The horse will quickly accept the rider's aids when this is done first in the walk. *The bend of the horse's body and the rider's aids are the same in all two-track figures.* The horse is bent evenly from poll to tail, either to the left or to the right; this is caused by the rider's pressing his leg against the horse's left or right side to bend the horse's body around the rider's left or right leg.

Only in the traversal and in leg-yielding does the horse perform on distinct two-tracks; that is, the front legs and the hind legs move on separate tracks. Here, too, leg-yielding helps a great deal to train the horse to bend his body, and can also be used as a correcting aid if the horse is losing impulsion and is slipping away from the rider's aids. Leg-yielding is also helpful to prevent the horse from shying or to enable the rider to position the horse in order to open or close a gate. If a horse tips his head and carries one ear lower than the other, for example the right ear, it is proof of lack of flexibility in the right hip joint and the rib cage. Only leg-yielding can correct this. If it is not corrected, the rider will encounter resistance in the counterchanges and flying changes to the left as well as in the development of the pirouettes to both sides.

Riders who are ambitious and willing to learn the art of riding should use leg-yielding as an aid to help the horse become accustomed to going on two-tracks and to make the horse responsive and flexible to the rider's aids. Once a horse is responsive, the rider can use the same aids not only if the horse resists, but also if he is disobedient. To punish or to discipline a horse is wrong and absolutely unnecessary if the rider has observed the unwritten law of nature under which every horse and rider has to work, and if the rider's proper training methods have made the horse supple and flexible by practicing the appropriate exercises. Otherwise, the rider will be the loser because of the greater physical strength of the horse. Also, the rider will not be able to train his horse to be a successful Grand Prix horse.

During this training period, the rider must give the horse a rest by riding cross-country in the ordinary gaits. By using this type of riding, the rider can avoid fatiguing the horse's muscles.

All exercises on two-tracks improve the flexibility of all of the joints, particularly the joints of the hind legs which are necessary for the horse to push himself forward and sideward, and which make it possible for the horse to move elastically in regular, cadenced steps and strides.

The rider must make the horse canter on two-tracks as well, first on the long side of the ring or riding area. The horse will become accustomed to this in a short period of time by being able to canter haunches-in. When the horse can canter on the long side he can and will do the same on the crossing line. The rider must practice this cantering in both directions until the horse is flexible enough to remain relaxed, balanced, collected, and in vigorous forward-sideward impulsion. The rider can overcome difficulties in the horse's *not* moving willingly sideward by influencing the

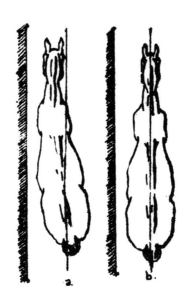

Crooked and straight horse.

horse with the same aids used in leg-yielding. There are the aids on the opposite side for the direction in which the horse is moving.

The rider must realize that all exercises in ordinary and strong paces and all exercises in collected and extended paces going on a single-track or on two-tracks are exercises to make a horse straight from poll to tail. Only then will the horse bend his spine evenly to the left or to the right. All four-legged animals move in a crooked line; horses move with the right hind leg to the right and with the left hind leg between the front legs. This gives the horse a so-called weak or strong side. The rider's obligation is to make the horse, through the exercises, evenly flexible to both sides, longitudinally as well as laterally.

Riders who have achieved this will not find it difficult for their horses to execute the flying change. Before the rider asks his horse to execute the flying change he should practice many simple changes of lead. Every horse trained to this point will respond willingly and quickly so that it will be easy to execute the flying change. If the rider has trained his horse to execute this figure in a relaxed and balanced manner, the horse will be able to respond willingly to very light aids. Before giving the aids for the flying change, the rider should be certain that the horse is in balance and light on rider's hands. The rider must be able to feel the horse bend to the side to which he is going to change. If the rider sits firm and steady, he will be able to feel the horse contract his back muscle to the left or right. Many changes will bring the horse to the stage where he is able to remain relaxed and balanced. The contact between the horse's mouth and the rider's hands will become very light. The rider should never interfere with his hands; he should practice the flying changes until he is able to *feel* the contraction of the horse's back muscles. The horse will then give the rider the correct bend from poll to tail by his own effort. A sensitive horse is inclined to swing his hind leg too far to the side to which he should change. In this case, the rider should spread his hands two hands apart. He will then be able to avoid the swinging. After a very short period of time, the rider will be able to guide the horse correctly through the figure in the walk, trot, and canter. He should then ride from the point of change to the center point and back to the point of change. In other words, from K to X and from X to H. These letters are used by the F.E.I. only to assist the translators. The rider should remember the sequence of the tests and not the letters. At the letter X, the rider should first ride the horse one step or stride straight forward and then change direction. In this way, the horse, in a short time, can perform correctly by going parallel to the long sides, leading slightly ahead with the shoulder, and then making the flying change perfectly straight. The rider has to train the horse so that he is responsive and sensitive to the aids before the rider is able to ride the counterchanges correctly.

When starting the counterchange in the canter, the rider should first ask for eight or ten strides to the left and to the right. In changes after eight strides, for example, the rider should ride straight after the seventh stride. It is simpler for the horse and rider to maintain balance this way. It is good for the rider to practice these changes first in the walk so that he and the horse become accustomed to the rapid change of direction and to the rapid influences the rider has to use to keep the horse relaxed, balanced, and collected. All horses should be able to perform the counterchange with very light contact between the rider's hands and the horse's mouth, and entirely on the rider's driving aids, as a result of their longitudinal and lateral flexibility.

In this stage of the training, the horse already responds very sensitively to the rider's weight. The rider has only to concentrate on pushing his inside knee down, thus putting more weight on the inside. The horse will willingly follow the rider's inside leg aid, and the pressure on the outside of his neck from the outside rein will help the horse maintain his balance. Frequent half-halts will keep the horse balanced and must be practiced often. Difficulties can arise when the horse is not responsive enough to the rider's outside aids. The rider can be very successful here by applying the same aids he uses in leg-yielding. Bending the horse to the outside temporarily will make the horse very responsive to the outside aids.

Horses who are able to perform well and accept the rider's aids willingly and responsively will also respond to the rider's aids going straight ahead. The rider should make his horse accustomed to the aids by first only asking for a flying change *after* the corner of the short side and again *before* the corner of the short side. The rider has to use very strong and distinct aids at first. Again, frequent half-halts will keep the horse balanced and relaxed.

After a short while, the rider will feel the horse respond to the pressure of his calves alone, especially when the horse responds by accepting the half-halt during the split second of suspension. *It is more the ability of the horse to keep his balance and to stay relaxed than it is the ability of the rider to apply the correct aids that makes the flying changes possible.* Horses which have been made flexible will show no difficulties and will not resist.

Once the horse can remain relaxed and balanced, it will not be difficult for the rider to ask the horse to execute the flying change slowly and more often—eight strides, six strides, four strides. When the rider receives this feeling from the horse, he can make the horse sensitive to the point where he will be able to ride the horse with one hand and ask for the flying

change while increasing and decreasing the paces. After the rider has patiently accomplished this, the horse
will be so responsive and flexible that he can keep the
sequence of the gait and canter almost on the place, if
the rider influences the horse to shorten his base of
support. The rider should ride these transitions also in
the trot and the walk from extended to collected paces
to almost on the place and vice versa. This makes the
horse able to perform the turn on the place—the pirouette. To execute the turn on the place, the rider must
bring his weight to the inside by pressing his inside
knee down. With the help of his braced back, used as a
lever, the rider will be able to keep the sequence and
regularity of the steps and strides and to turn by utiliz-
ing the pressure of the outside rein against the outside
of the horse's neck. In order to prepare the horse, the
rider must have the response of the horse to go shoulder-fore. When he has that response, he should ask for
the turn. If the rider wants to convince himself of the
horse's performance, he can also have the horse correctly execute the pirouette while holding the reins in
one hand.

It must be stressed that in all this training the rider's
seat has to be very firm and steady. A loose seat can
cause the horse to be out of balance. The further development of the horse's suppleness and flexibility, as
well as his relaxation, impulsion, and accuracy in
training and riding the F.E.I. tests, depend upon the
rider's seat. It cannot be stressed enough that only a
rider who is able to tighten and relax his own muscles
can influence and guide the horse properly. It must be
understood that a firm and steady seat does not mean
that the rider should sit rigid and stiff and use force by
hitting, kicking, or jerking a horse. The correct training, set forth in this book, will convince the rider of the
horse's suppleness and flexibility. At this point in
training, the rider must be able to ride the horse with

one hand on a single-track as well as on two-tracks. Only with this assurance of performance can the rider think about training of the horse further for the F.E.I. tests. Being able to ride a horse with one hand on single- and two-track figures is the unmistakable proof of the horse's balance, relaxation, and longitudinal and lateral flexibility. Without these, no rider has any chance to represent his country with honor in International or Olympic competition.

When the rider has reached this stage of training the horse, he can enjoyably improve the horse's suppleness and flexibility. The horse's mentality cannot be developed; it is the rider's intellect, used to give the horse the appropriate exercises, which makes it possible for the horse to go in a higher degree of collection. This is necessary for all paces and figures found in the F.E.I. tests. Because of the rapid succession of paces and figures, as well as the change of direction, the horse must be very flexible. These tests must be ridden completely relaxed, with vigorous impulsion and accuracy of all paces and figures. These, combined with natural balance, gaits, and beauty, make it worthwhile to contnue the training of the horse. *Only the quality of all of this together is decisive for good scoring and placement in International and Olympic competition.*

Patiently and intelligently, the rider should now start with the piaffe. The rider can decide which method of training he prefers. He is the one who feels the movements of the horse, and only he can judge which approach is correct for that particular horse. The inexperienced rider needs the help of an expert. It is of the utmost importance that the horse maintain the sequence of the trot movement and bend his hip joint. This enables the horse to move in rhythm, elastically, with a spring-like and undulating motion forward—without covering much ground. Developing this is very time consuming, and should be practiced and im-

The transition from the collected trot to the piaffe. *(Photograph by Arnold Weiner.)*

proved slowly *every* day, but only for a *short* period of time. The rider should be satisfied with a few steps daily until the horse is accustomed to it. Properly done, the development of the piaffe can be used as a suppling exercise to achieve a higher degree of collection. This makes it more enjoyable for the horse and rider to develop both in order to achieve the highest standard as required under F.E.I. rules. Until the horse is able to perform the piaffe exactly in place, the rider should be certain that the horse is gaining ground in order to maintain impulsion. The horse which is able to lower the croup by bending the hip joint and relaxing the back will erect himself and stay very light on the rider's hands.

The rider must realize that he has no influence whatsoever on how high the horse will lift his legs. It is irritating to the horse when the rider tries to urge the horse to lift his legs higher by tapping them with a whip, especially the front legs, as is suggested by some trainers. *The height that a horse lifts his legs is entirely dependent on the horse's ability.* Some are able to lift the diagonal pair of legs higher than others. The importance lies in the regularity of the steps, the lowering of the croup, and the erection of the forehand, as well as the elevation in the piaffe and passage. *The piaffe and the passage are very individual movements, and are different for each horse.* It is advisable not to perform the passage until the horse is trained to perform the paces and figures for the Grand Prix level test. It is then extremely easy to ask the horse to go more forward in the piaffe until he is able to find his balance, and steps elastically and with spring-like grace from one diagonal to the other. This, too, must be alternated with the extended trot. In a short time the horse can perform the extended trot, the passage, and the piaffe and then go back to the passage and back from the passage to the piaffe.

Transition from the piaffe to the passage.

All of these figures should also be practiced on the bridlepath, especially when returning to the stable. The necessary impulsion is then naturally forthcoming from the horse and should be accepted by the rider until he has the piaffe and the passage perfected. Once the horse has found his balance and is flexible enough, it is not difficult for him to perform these two figures. The rider should sit very firm in the saddle, and should influence the horse with strong driving aids. He should never try to help the horse by moving his body—this will impair the horse's impulsion, which is needed to move forward in cadence. It must be stressed that the rider should not allow himself to become so intent on this concentrated work that he forgets to rest the horse by walking him occasionally with a long rein. He must always keep in mind that he makes the horse's muscles work the most. The flexibility of the horse's skeletal system is developed through the action of the horse's muscles.

Another way to achieve the piaffe is to prepare the horse in hand. This is not recommended for inexperienced riders. For them, it is better and easier to slowly shorten the base of support in the trot. Horses which can go in the extended trot can be brought to the collected trot and from the collected trot to shorter steps. The rider must be satisfied with very few steps at first, and must always then ride forward with great impulsion. This, too, can be done successfully on the bridlepath on the return to the stable. The rider should limber up the horse while riding away from the stable. He can then use the natural impulsion of the horse to his own advantage. All horses have a very good sense of direction, and it is their habit to give the rider the impulsion needed for the execution of the piaffe when returning to the stable.

The piaffe is most important. From this figure the horse can be trained to move relaxed in the trot movement and almost on the place, forward. He will lower his croup, and the rider will easily feel it if the horse remains relaxed and balanced. *A horse properly trained in the piaffe will remain relaxed and balanced in all other paces and figures.* As mentioned before, the piaffe can be used as a suppling exercise for all paces and figures in high collection. The development of the piaffe is time consuming and the rider must employ great patience. It will be very advantageous to spend the time to perfect the piaffe. *The piaffe is perfect if the horse moves with a gentle swinging up and down motion of his spine and contracts and expands his back muscles due to his flexible joints.* A horse should *not* show an up and down bounce of his body—only tension and stiffness causes this. The horse's body (that is, the rump, head, and neck) should remain steady and the rhythm should be very pronounced but relaxed. The rider can now influence the horse to execute the piaffe in the left or right position and exactly on the place. When the horse shows resistance, the rider can be certain that the necessary longitudinal and lateral flexibility has not been established. More transitions and work on two-tracks are advisable, and the rider can try again in a relatively short time to execute this figure. He should never try to overcome the horse's resistance to the piaffe by disciplining the horse. This is true in all further development for the F.E.I. tests. In general, it takes one year to perfect the piaffe and the passage.

In this stage of training, the rider is able to feel the improved strong back muscles of the horse and the flexibility of all the joints. The rider can now also bring the horse to perfection in the piaffe and the passage. Many transitions, by increasing and decreasing the paces alternated with the piaffe and the passage, are very helpful in bringing the horse to complete relaxation and balance. Regardless of the sequence of the figures in the test, the rider is now able to ride any described test. Long relaxing rides on the bridle path are not only a necessity to keep the horse's and the rider's physical condition, but are also a great joy and pleasure. The rider has the opportunity to practice all paces and figures separately while riding outdoors. He improves not only the strength of the horse's muscles, but can also make the horse's joints more flexible. By riding outdoors, the rider can avoid the horse's training becoming a routine and the horse will then perform only if the rider is using his aids to influence the horse to execute certain paces and figures.

The rider must practice the transitions and must be certain that the horse maintains the sequence of his gaits while shortening and lengthening the base of support. Many transitions in all two-tracks, going from one position to the other, will greatly improve the horse's longitudinal and lateral flexibility. In this way, the horse cannot learn to anticipate the figures. He will be trained to accept and to respond only to the rider's aids. The rider can make the horse very sensitive to his aids so that he is able to ride with entirely invisible aids. A horse must perform the tests in complete relaxation and balance under F.E.I. requirements.

At this point in the horse's training, to convince himself that the horse is performing properly in a relaxed and balanced manner, the rider should ride as often and for as long as possible with the reins in one hand. If he has accomplished this on a suitable horse he can rest assured that he and the horse are ready to successfully compete in the stiffest competition.

A rider who wants to compete in the F.E.I. tests must understand that he and his horse have to practice the gymnastic exercises described in this book daily to be able to compete with the selected riders and horses of other countries. These tests are written by the F.E.I. Dressage Commission, which consists of experts from

Passage.

different countries. The rider who has trained his horse methodically and gymnastically will not only improve his driving seat, but will also be able to influence the horse correctly.

The horse which can perform tests A, B, and C in a relaxed and balanced manner is properly trained to execute the figures under the F.E.I. rules. Test D is a substitute test for the Saint George (the simplest of the F.E.I. tests), Intermediare, and the Grand Prix, so that the rider does not have to ride the same tests as in F.E.I. The rider should not ride the same tests repeatedly, as this will cause the horse to anticipate the figures.

The substitute tests are more difficult for the rider, but he will subsequently find that it is easier for himself and the horse to perform in International competition.

In the F.E.I. tests the horse has to make the transitions willingly and smoothly from collected to extended gaits, and from one direction and figure to another in rapid succession. Only a horse which is supple and flexible will perform these tests in a relaxed and balanced manner, with harmony and grace. The rider can achieve the degree of high collection necessary to execute the tests only with his driving aids, even while decreasing the gaits. If he neglects this, the horse will lose impulsion and cadence. The judges will always score sufficient points or less points, according to the horse's performance.

It is imperative that the rider keep the horse light on the bit and relaxed and balanced *at all times.*

During the training period the rider must be certain that the horse is flexible enough to collect himself by accepting the rider's driving aids. Once the horse responds calmly and willingly to the rider's aids, the rider can start to ask for the flying change after eight or ten strides. When the horse can execute this figure in a

Collected Trot.

relaxed and balanced manner, the rider can ask for the change after four strides, then three strides, then two strides. Most horses respond willingly, but need some time to be able to keep their balance. When a horse does not remain balanced and on the aids, the rider must give half-halts to re-establish balance and not ask for this figure again until the horse is on the aids. Only after the horse responds to the rider's aids and remains relaxed, balanced, and attentive during the execution of the flying changes as described above can the rider ask for a change on every stride. It is imperative that the horse keep his balance in order to be able to change after each stride. Almost all horses need a long time to be able to respond. The rider has to give the aids after each stride, during the suspension. The rider should ask for the flying change only when the horse is light on the bit. In the beginning, the aids must be strong and distinct when asking the horse to execute this figure.

For most horses, it is easier to execute the change from the left to the right. The rider has to find this out. As soon as the horse executes the flying change after every stride in a calm, relaxed, and balanced manner, the rider should ask for changes on every stride more frequently along the long side of the training ring. At this point, the rider should allow the horse to relax by walking. The best procedure is to ask for the changes on one long side of the ring and to walk on the other long side of the ring. When a horse is able to execute the flying change after every stride for the full length of the long side of the ring, the rider should be able to keep the horse on the aids and in balance. Every horse can be brought to such a a responsive state that he changes with completely invisible aids. It is not difficult to keep a horse straight during the flying changes if the rider asks for them in serpentines and allows the horse to go straight before crossing the centerline. The

Extended Trot. Mr. Otto Loerke on *Afrika,* holding the reins in one hand. *(Foto-Tiedemann.)*

horse is now accustomed to the aids and is flexible enough to remain on the straight. This figure can be practiced on the bridlepath because the horse naturally keeps his impulsion and is more attentive to the rider's aids and does not anticipate the command for this figure. If the horse willingly executes the flying change on every stride, an important gesture on the part of the rider is to immediately stop riding, dismount, and try again the next day.

The counterchanges, or zig-zag traverse, in the trot and canter need the attention of the rider. It is important for the horse and rider to remember that the shoulders of the horse must lead slightly ahead of the hindquarters, and that the horse should move parallel to the wall. The horse will position his hindquarters ahead, especially during the change of direction, if the rider uses his outside leg too early or too strongly. The rider has to practice the counterchanges in the walk before he acquires the proper feeling necessary to ask the horse to obey his aids. The rider must be able to feel the horse contract his back muscles to the left or to the right.

Another figure required in the F.E.I. tests is the piaffe. The development of the piaffe and passage can and should be done while the rider prepares the horse for the Saint George and Intermediare tests, and should be started as soon as the horse moves willingly forward in half steps. This figure should be practiced every day for a few minutes, as it requires great physical effort from both horse and rider. Performing the piaffe and passage is not as difficult as is generally thought. However, it takes great patience on the rider's part not to excite the horse during this training period. The horse must be completely relaxed and completely balanced to respond to the rider's aids. In the beginning, the rider should be satisfied with a few steps and should ride well forward in an extended trot before trying the figure again. Until the horse is able to execute the piaffe in place, he has to be trained to stay relaxed by moving slightly forward with diagonal steps. This forward movement is necessary for the horse to keep his impulsion. The rider should not try to help the horse by moving his upper body or legs. This will cause the horse to lose his balance and, consequently, he will lose the forward impulsion which is extremely important for proper executon of the piaffe and the passage. It is imperative that the rider constantly remember that the horse needs the guidance of the rider's strong forward driving seat to achieve forward impulsion. The more collection the rider asks from the horse, the stronger the driving aids must be to influence the horse. The rider must improve the execution of the piaffe to such a degree that he feels the horse lower his croup by bending his hip joint. Only then can the horse bend his hind legs in the hocks. The driving seat enables the rider to feel the gentle up-and-down swinging of the horse's spine and the alternate contraction of the horse's muscles. Due to the high degree of collection, the rider will feel the horse's hind and front feet move up and down in a very pronounced and very strong rhythm—this is cadence in its greatest and purest form. The rider who has trained the horse to this degree of perfection is able to use the piaffe as a suppling exercise, which will enable the horse to be completely relaxed and balanced in all gaits and figures. This work requires great effort on the horse's part and should be gradually asked for by the rider for longer and more frequent periods of time. Only then will the rider be able to train his horse to perform the F.E.I. tests with no visible aids. The horse will remain relaxed, with great impulsion, and with complete balance on the aids.

Because of the horse's longitudinal and lateral flexibility at this point, the rider can now ask the horse to maintain the sequence of his gaits in all transitions, from the most extended to the most collected (as in the pirouette or the piaffe), whether in walk, trot, or canter.

The half-pirouette must be practiced many times, especially in the walk. A rider should often ride the transition from extended to collected walk so that he can turn the horse on the haunches and the horse will keep his hind legs moving as though he were moving straight forward. In the canter, the rider has to practice the same way, but before he asks the horse to turn he must be able to canter almost in place, allowing the horse to cover enough ground to keep the sequence of his stride. Many transitions from the extended to the collected canter are necessary to make it possible for the horse to maintain his impulsion. As soon as the rider feels that the horse is losing impulsion he should increase the pace to the extended canter. In a short time the rider will feel the response of the horse. He can then turn, in the beginning allowing the horse to make only a small circle with his hind legs, before he asks the horse to remain in place, setting the inside hind leg down where it left the ground. A properly trained horse, which is longitudinally as well as laterally flexible, will accept the aids from the rider to maintain the shoulder-fore position in the canter as well as in the transitions. It is of great importance for the horse to keep his balance and for the rider to be able to ask the horse to use the inside hind leg in executing the pirouette. If the horse loses his impulsion, the rider should re-establish it before he again asks the horse to execute this figure.

In shoulder-in, haunches-in, haunches-out, or traversals to the center point and back to the track, the rider will feel the horse contract his back muscles and bend his neck with very little help from the rider's hands. Should the horse lean on one rein to one side, the rider has to use the opposite leg to correct this.

Most horses do not accept bending to the left; the rider therefore has to use his right leg so that the horse bends his spine and ribs more to the left.

A horse trained in the exercises from this book will become very sensitive and responsive to the rider's aids. Therefore, it is the obligation of the rider to strictly observe the horse's law of nature. Excitable and temperamental horses have to be treated and handled accordingly. Long rides on the bridlepath, during which the rider can give the horse all the suppling and collecting exercises he needs, are not merely helpful, but are very important. Phlegmatic horses also should be ridden on the bridlepath—more brisk, forward riding keeps them limber. This is very important for the rider also. He must keep himself in excellent physical condition to be able to ride the horse with completely invisible aids. The rides on the bridlepath will give him ample opportunity to improve his riding technique so that the horse will respond to the aids sensibly and sensitively.

It is most important that the rider not start to collect the horse before the horse is limbered, completely relaxed, and accepts the rider's driving aids in all ordinary and strong gaits. *It is advisable that the rider also ask the horse for all exercises on a single- or two-tracks in the ordinary walk, trot, and canter. This will give the rider the guarantee that the horse will perform all collected gaits and paces harmoniously, energetically, gracefully, and in cadence forward.* In this way, the rider will be able to find out how much warming up time he and the horse need to ride through the test, regardless of which level test the horse is going to perform. *This is of utmost importance in riding the F.E.I. tests.*

Chapter X

Conclusion

Many riders will probably ask why I so often mention the guidelines and tests published by the Advisory Committee. In my opinion, it seems appropriate to examine both the old and new tests, so that every instructor and rider can come to his own conclusions about what we can do to improve our training methods.

Our present tests emphasize figures, which a horse can only perform after it is going well forward on the rider's aids. For instance, we start in the first level with a figure calling for a turn to the right in the middle of the first long side and to the left on the opposite long side. To be correct, every turn must be ridden in a quarter-volt. However, at this stage the horse is not flexible enough to do this, and without leg-yielding he cannot be responsive to the rider's legs; the frequently seen use of draw reins and chambons is proof of this. These reins must sometimes be used on difficult horses, but never by inexperienced riders. The figure in question was taken from a book in which the author describes the training of horses for exhibition purposes. The training differs from training designed to develop the natural ability of the horse in order to com-

Mr. S. Eilatov on *Absinth*.

pete under F.E.I. rules and regulations, although the terminology is the same. In training to compete under International rules and regulations the horse must not only execute the figures, but every step and stride in all gaits, paces, and figures must also be executed in the correct sequence of the walk, trot, and canter. This can only be accomplished with a training routine designed to improve the suppleness and flexibility of the horse and to coordinate the aids of the rider. Any interference from the rider's hands in the early stages will make this impossible. It can be done by the rider only with his driving aids, *i.e.,* his legs and back. This is possible only through leg-yielding.

The question here is: How can a rider train his horse from behind to the front and how can a rider influence his horse to bend his spine and ribs evenly from poll to tail? It certainly does not concern whether leg-yielding is a classical, performing, or baroque movement. It is a fact that leg-yielding is the most important exercise through which any rider can limber up the horse's trunk and make the horse responsive and sensitive to his legs. Every rider can then influence his horse to bend evenly from poll to tail, especially when the horse should be trained to look in the direction in which it is moving. A horse which is not trained to yield to the rider's legs will not bend its spine and ribs when the rider wants to bend his horse around his inside leg by taking his outside leg slightly back. The horse will also not bend its spine and ribs evenly in the split second during suspension in the canter in order to execute the flying change correctly.

The new tests also do not make it possible for the rider to develop and improve the horse's forward impulsion, because there are too many figures in all tests. This is the reason why many horses are not performing in self-carriage and are giving the impression of being forcefully pressed together. These horses also move either too slowly or too fast instead of moving in a collected or extended manner by maintaining the same rhythm in cadence. This is due to a misinterpretation of "riding with great impulsion forward." Instructors and riders must understand that horses should lengthen the base of support in the extended gaits and paces by lengthening the steps and strides, and not by increasing the rhythm.

For these reasons, no rider can train his horse properly in the way in which our four levels are now formulated. The foundations are not properly laid for the horse and rider to accurately reach the fifth level. The present fifth level is literally translated from the German Grand Prix, while the D3 test of the Advisory Committee is a logical ending to *all* tests.

Without leg-yielding, the rider will only provoke unnecessary resistance in the horse and consequent punishment by the rider. In my experience, this is not at all necessary, although it does not mean that the rider should ride his horse passively. He will sometimes have to be strict, but he should never punish his horse. The rider should reward his horse often, but punishment is avoidable if the horse is obedient to the rider's legs. This obedience also makes it possible for the rider to give half-halts. He should give these to keep his horse relaxed, balanced, and attentive to his aids, especially by decreasing the gaits and paces. Through leg-yielding, the training of a horse is made more enjoyable for both horse and rider, and it will be more effective and successful in the long term.

The rider's back is also important in executing leg-yielding and in giving half-halts. A hollow and/or rounded back is ineffective. Only when the rider can use his back as a lever can he get the horse to stay light and erect on the bit. By squeezing his legs, bracing his back, and fixing his hands he can slow his horse down when it quickens its steps and strides and he can also keep the impulsion by decreasing the gaits and paces. In this way, the rider's hands will never work against and interfere with the horse's impulsion.

Therefore, a horse must be made responsive to the rider's legs and to the half-halts before the rider can guide his horse with his driving aids through all of the exercises in the first and second stages of the training routine. This is the meaning of the expression "the horse is on the rider's aids." The Advisory Committee issued the A, B, C, and D tests so that all riders could learn to guide their horses with these driving aids. The number of figures was gradually increased through the three A tests and the three B tests to include all figures a horse can perform on a single-track. Instructors and riders should realize that in the F.E.I. tests all figures are the same—the sole difference is that the horse must perform these tests in collected gaits, paces, and figures on a single- and two-tracks. In the new tests, this is not clearly stated.

The Advisory Committee's guidelines also formulated the change of direction across the ring as "to move from one side to the other" instead of "change rein," which came to us from England. We also thought the term traversal to be more distinct and appropriate than the terms two-tracking or half-pass because traversal means "the act of traversing, to go across on two-tracks."

The new tests also do not clearly separate the training routine between the first and second stages. The tests of the first stage should make it possible for the rider to develop the ability of the horse's hind legs to push forward with great impulsion. In the second stage the rider can then influence his horse to use this power to push and to combine this with the capacity to carry more of its own and the rider's weight on its hind

Mrs. E. Petushkova-Brumel on *Pepel.*

legs in order to execute the collected gaits in cadence. This will automatically lower the croup and lighten the forehand.

All of the fourth level tests we now have are not stepping stones to train a horse to the fifth level. The tests prepared by the Advisory Committee served as a sound basis for the next levels because they incorporated riding with one hand in almost all tests. Through riding with the reins in one hand, the rider can convince himself how well relaxed, balanced, supple, and flexible his horse has become.

The Advisory Committee also wanted to emphasize that dressage is not discipline, nor is it a wrestling match between horse and rider. All riders must keep in mind that it is not important that a horse and rider can execute the required figures. The whole composition of all gaits, paces, and figures is decisive for good scoring. In the Grand Prix test the horse must give the impression that it is performing entirely on its own effort. This is not possible with the composition of the new tests because they lead riders to drill and mechanize their horses and not to develop the horse's natural ability.

The establishment of a National institution will not be the solution. The cavalry schools of other nations have never competed successfully with correctly trained dressage horses. Only properly designed guidelines can make it possible for riders to individually train their horses. Each rider must individualize the training of each horse he trains; this is the only successful method of training and developing each horse's particular ability either for jumping, eventing, or dressage. The tests and guidelines formulated by the Advisory Committee make it possible for all riders to train their horses to the highest degree of relaxation, balance, suppleness, and flexibility.

Appendix I

Excerpts from *Notes on Dressage*
Published 1952
Prepared by the U.S. Equestrian Advisory
Committee
Chairman—General Guy V. Henry

DEFINITION OF GAITS ON A SINGLE- AND TWO-
TRACKS
Every rider has to realize that a horse can only
lengthen and shorten his base of support.

Ordinary Walk—The ordinary walk must be free and
regular with a long step. The horse walks lightly but
calmly, with an even, deliberate step, clearly marking
four beats equally spaced and very distinct. The rider
maintains a constant soft contact with the horse's
mouth. The horse's hind hoofs must step in the footprints of the forelegs.

Strong Walk—The horse should cover as much ground
as he can without haste and without losing the regularity of his steps. The hind feet touch the ground clearly
in the prints of the fore feet. The rider lets the horse

stretch out his head and neck without, however, losing contact in such a way that at any movement he can make the horse change his pace, speed, or direction.

Collected Walk—By lowering the hindquarters the horse lightens the forehand while maintaining his mobility. He moves freely and with regular steps. Each step covers less ground than in the ordinary walk but is higher, since the joints articulate more. However, the forward impuslion is clearly apparent. Steps bearing a resemblance to pacing are incorrect and reveal that the rider is influencing too strongly with his hands and not enough with his legs. The hind hoofs must step in the footprints of the front feet.

(Extended) Free Walk—The rider lets the reins slide through to the buckle allowing him complete freedom of head and neck.

Ordinary Trot (Natural, as normally used in road work)—The horse goes forward freely and straight, goes well off his hocks, softly into his bridle, with a balanced and free action. The steps should be even and the hind feet should step exactly in the tracks of the fore feet.

Strong Trot—This is a pace to be executed before the horse is sufficiently trained to be asked for a correct extended trot, i.e., before the training has reached a sufficiently advanced stage to produce the impulsion of the hind legs necessary for the Extended Trot. It must lengthen the steps and the hind legs step clearly ahead of the forelegs.

Collected Trot—The neck is raised, thus enabling the shoulders to move with greater ease in all directions, the hocks being well engaged and maintaining energetic impulsion, notwithstanding the slower movement. The horse's steps are shorter, but he is

Ordinary Trot.

Strong Trot.

Collected Trot.

Extended Trot.

more mobile and lighter, the beat more pronounced. The hind legs must step in the footprints of the front legs.

Extended Trot—The horse lengthens the step without getting out of hand, extends his neck and, as the result of great impulsion from the quarters, uses his shoulders to cover more ground at each step without his action becoming much higher. The beat is more pronounced.

Ordinary Canter (Natural, as normally used in road work)—The horse, perfectly straight from the poll to the tail, moves freely with a natural stride and balance.

Strong Canter—The same as for the Strong Trot (without haste). The horse must lengthen the strides.

Collected Canter—The shoulders are supple, free, and mobile and the quarters very active. The horse goes with a more pronounced swing and undiminished impulsion.

Extended Canter—The horse extends his neck; the tip of the nose points more or less forward, the horse lengthens his stride without losing any of his calm and lightness, always without haste, but the beat becomes pronounced.

Flying Change of Lead—This should be executed without hesitation, in graceful, vigorous strides. The rider's aids should be invisible. Hind and front legs must change simultaneously "in the air" during the moment of suspension which follows each stride at the canter. The horse remains absolutely straight, calm, and light.

Piaffe or Trot-in-Place—Since the piaffe is an individual gait, every horse will show a slightly different way of performing it. Some horses will show higher action, some less; also many horses have to move a lit-

Extended trot with reins in one hand.

Collected Canter.

tle forward. Characteristic of every correct piaffe is the lowering of the hindquarters, the regularity of the steps, the cadence, the supple motion of the back, the erection of the neck and head. Bobbing up and down of the croup or body, or balancing from side to side behind, is proof of stiff legs and back and especially shows that the horse is incapable of bending his hip joints. In addition to these faults in the incorrectly suppled horse there will generally be an unsteady connection between the rider's hand and the horse's mouth. In other words, the horse moves his head up and down, goes behind the bit or against the rider's hand, but does not really have his balance and so is not capable of staying steady on the bit.

Passage—This is a slow, shortened, very lofty, and cadenced trot. It is characterized by a more accentuated flexion of knees and hocks and by the graceful elasticity of the movement. Each diagonal pair of legs, well together, is raised and put to the ground alternately, gaining little ground and with an even cadence and a prolonged moment of suspension. In principle, the toe of the raised foreleg should be level with the middle of the cannon bone of the other foreleg. The toe of the raised hind leg should be very slightly lower and should reach above the fetlock joint of the other hind leg.

The same passage cannot be expected of all horses. Depending upon conformation and temperament, as well as the energy derived from their impulsion, some horses have a more rounded and roomier action, others a more lively and shorter action. Swinging the quarters from one side to the other is considered a fault.

Transitions—The transitions from one gait to another, or from one pace to another, should be clear and quick but smooth and supple. Gait or pace must be maintained to the exact point where the horse is required to

Transition from the collected trot to the piaffe.

change. There must be a clearly visible distinction between the different paces of a gait. The horse must
keep his self-carriage and lightness on the bit. From
collected to extended gaits the horse should show
graceful motion and a balanced carriage and cadence.
From extended gaits to collected gaits the same degree
of forward impulsion must be evident, even in the
high collected gaits like piaffe, passage, and pirouette.

FIGURES ON TWO-TRACKS

Two-Tracks—The aim of two-track movements is to bring the balance and the pace into harmony. They supple all parts of the horse, especially increasing the suppleness of the quarters and joints, and freedom of the shoulders. They also make the horse more obedient to the aids of the rider. They should only be practiced for a short time and always be followed by some energetic movement straight forward. In these movements the horse is bent uniformly from poll to tail and moves with the forehand and hindquarters on two distinct tracks. The proper bending of the horse's body is the key to the correctness of the training. The distance between the tracks should not be more than one step. The pace remains always regular, supple, and free, maintained by a constant impulsion; this is often lost because the rider is preoccupied with the bend of the horse only. In two-track movements the forehand should always be in advance of the quarters.

Leg-yielding—This is the primary lesson for the horse in yielding to the pressure of the rider's legs. It should be executed at a 45 degree angle to whatever track the horse is traveling. The horse is slightly bent in his entire length toward the side of the rider's active leg. The fore and hind legs on this side *cross in front of the others.* Leg-yielding is the foundation of all other figures on two-tracks.

In the following two-track movements the horse must not be at an angle greater than 30 to 35 degrees to the direction in which he is moving.

Shoulder-In—The neck is bent in the opposite direction from which he is moving. The horse should be bent evenly from poll to tail to the inside. The inside leg follows the same track as the outside front leg; the forward motion is marked; *the legs do not cross.*

Haunches-In—The horse is bent in the direction in which he is traveling. The horse should be bent evenly from poll to tail to the inside. The outside hind leg follows the same track as the inside front leg; the forward movement is marked; *the legs do not cross.*

Two-Tracks on the Diagonal (Traversal or Pass)—The horse moves on two-tracks, but progresses on the diagonal rather than straight ahead. There is a slight bending of the horse's body toward the direction in which he is going, and the forehand slightly precedes the hindquarters.

If the rider tries to move more sideward than forward in two-tracking, he does so at the expense of the forward impulsion. Dragging hind legs and lack of vigorous forward movement are proof of insufficient collection and insufficient bending of the hip joint. Unevenness in the gaits and heaviness of the forehand will be the result. In all two-track figures the horse should show a response to the rider's weight aids; the rider should lead the horse almost imperceptibly with his weight.

Appendix II

Excerpts from the Rules and Regulations of the
F.E.I.
(Fédération Equestrienne Internationale)

ARTICLE 100   PURPOSE OF THE REGULATIONS AND
RULES

1   The General Regulations and Rules are established so that competitors from different nations may compete against each other under fair and equal conditions. If there is any doubt about the meaning of these regulations, they should be interpreted in the sense of providing fair conditions for all competitors.

2   All events referred to in the Regulations may only be organized by countries whose NFs (National Federations) are affiliated to the F.E.I. and only competitors whose NFs are affiliated to the F.E.I. may take part.

3   The Regulations govern all international eques-

trian events organized by or on behalf of the F.E.I. The Rules governing each particular discipline must be read in conjunction with the Regulations.

4 These Regulations have been drawn up in the broadest possible spirit so as to allow organizing committees the fullest freedom in the management of their events and in the preparation of their programs.

ARTICLE 101 PURPOSES

1 The purposes of the F.E.I. are as follows:
(a) to be the sole international authority for the equestrian sports of Dressage, Jumping, Competitions in the Open, Combined Competition, Three Day Events, Driving, and any other forms of equestrian sport which the General Assembly may from time to time decide to include;
(b) to promote the organization of international equestrian competition throughout the world;
(c) to coordinate, standardize and publish the rules and to supervise the organization of international equestrian events, while allowing the NFs the widest possible freedom in the arrangement of their programs;
(d) to standardize and approve the rules and programs for Championships, Olympic, and Regional Games and to control their technical organization;
(e) to provide the means for discussion and understanding between NFs, to give them support and encouragement and to strengthen their authority and prestige;
(f) to encourage instruction in riding, driving, and horsemanship for recreational purposes.

Dressage Events

ARTICLE 418   INTRODUCTION

All international Dressage Events, without exception, are held according to the rules given in the following articles.

ARTICLE 419   OBJECT OF THE INTERNATIONAL DRESSAGE EVENT

In instituting, in 1929, an international Dressage Event, the F.E.I. aimed to preserve the equestrian Art from the abuses to which it can be exposed and to preserve it in the purity of its principles, so that it could be handed on intact to generations of riders to come. There are three successive phases in the study of equitation. Each of these is the subject of a competition.

ARTICLE 420   TESTS

These tests, three in number, recognized Dressage tests of the F.E.I. are as follows:

1   Prix St. Georges. Competition of medium difficulty. The test of the Prix St. Georges is that of the middle stage of training. It comprises exercises to show the horse's submission to all the demands of the execution of classical equitation and a standard of physical development, which will enable him to carry them out with suppleness and lightness and without unnecessary effort.

2.   Intermediate Dressage Competition. Competition of advanced difficulty.

The object of the test of this competition is to lead horses on, progressively, and without harm to their organism, from the correct execution of the Prix St. Georges to the greater difficulties of the Grand Prix.

3. Grand Prix. Expert Competition. The Grand
   Prix is a competition of artistic equitation,
   which brings out the horse's perfect lightness,
   characterized by the total absence of resistance, and the complete development of
   impulsion. The test includes all the school
   paces and all the fundamental airs of the
   classical high school, of which the fantastic
   paces, based on extension of the forelegs, are
   no part (these are the leaps above the ground).
   For this reason the school leaps, obsolete in a
   great many countries, do not figure in the
   Grand Prix test.

Appendix III

Excerpts from the Fort Riley Cavalry School Manual

The intelligent operation and care of any mechanism is based on a good working knowledge of its general structure and normal functions. The animal body may be considered as a complex machine of many parts with each of these various parts normally functioning in a more or less integral structure of the animal body known as "anatomy." The science which treats the normal functioning of the animal body is known as "physiology." It is quite essential that the study of animal management include a basic knowledge of the anatomy and physiology of the horse so that the student may more intelligently recognize the facts upon which the fundamental principles of animal management are based. In this text, the study of anatomy and physiology will be correlated as much as possible and limited to those parts of greatest essential interest. The body of the horse is in general structure quite like the body of man. The chief differences are in the relative size and relationships of the various parts, and for these reasons the various structures of the horse will, in many instances, be compared with similar parts of the human body. The body of the horse, like that of man, is made up of a skeletal system, a muscular system, a digestive system, a respiratory system, a circulatory system, a urinary system, a nervous system, a reproductive system, and an outer covering of skin and hair.

SKELETAL SYSTEM

The skeletal system includes the bones and the ligaments which bind the bones together to form joints. The skeletal system gives the body form; rigidity. It forms bony cavities for the protection of vital organs. The bones and joints together form a complex system of levers and pulleys which, combined with the muscular system, gives the body the power of motion. The relative size and position of the bones determine the form or conformation of the horse and his efficiency for any particular work. The "trunk" or "axial skeleton" consists of the "skull," "spinal" or "vertebral column," "ribs," and "breast bones." The "limbs," forming the "appendicular skeleton," support the body and furnish the levers of propulsion.

Bones—The skeleton of the horse is made up of about 205 bones. In their living state, bones are composed of about one part organic matter and two parts inorganic matter. The latter, which is mineral matter, is largely lime salts. The bones, as you see them in a mounted skeleton, have been freed of organic matter and are white and brittle, but living bone is about twice as strong as a green oak stick of the same size. Bones, according to their shape, are classified as "long," "short," "fat," and "irregular."

"Long" bones are found in the limbs. They support

the body weight and act as the levers of propulsion.

"Short" bones occur chiefly in the knee and hock. They function in the dissipation of concussion.

"Flat" bones, such as the ribs, scapula, and some of the bones of the skull, help to enclose cavities containing vital organs.

"Irregular bones" are unpaired bones such as the vertebrae and some bones of the skull.

All bones, except at their points of articulation, are covered with a thin, tough, adherent membrane called "periosteum." It protects the bone and influences the growth of the bone to of certain extent. This latter function is of particular interest for we know that injury to this membrane often results in an abnormal bony growth called an "exotosis," occurring at the point of injury. Bony growths, such as splints, spavins, and ringbones, are the frequent result of some form of injury of the periosteum. The bone is, in part, nourished through blood vessels in the periosteum and there are many nerve endings in this membrane.

The articular or joint surfaces of bones are covered with a dense, very smooth, blush-colored substance called "cartilage." The cartilage diminishes the effects of concussion and provides a smooth joint surface offering a minimum of frictional resistance to movement.

Vertebral or Spinal Column—The vertebral or spinal column may be regarded as the basis of the skeleton from which all other parts originate. It is composed of irregularly shaped bones bound together with ligaments and cartilage, and forms a column of bones from the base of the skull to the tip of the tail. Through the length of this column there is an elongated cavity called the "spinal canal" that contains the "spinal cord," the main trunkline of nerves coming from the brain. Through this more or less flexible column of bones the powerful impetus of propulsion originating in the hind legs is transmitted to the forequarters of the animal. Indirectly, the vertebral column bears the weight of the rider and his equipment. The bones of the vertebral column are divided into five groups.

The "cervical," or neck, group contains seven "cervical vertebrae." The first of these, the "atlas," is jointed to the cranium by a hinge-like joint permitting only extension and flexion of the head on the neck. The next cervical vertebra is known as the "axis" and is so jointed to the atlas that it permits rotation of the head and atlas on the remainder of the neck. The remaining five cervical vertebrae have no special names. The column of bones in this region is arranged, when viewed from the side, in an S-shaped curve. Lengthening and shortening the neck is brought about by increasing or decreasing this curvature. The cervical group is the most flexible part of the vertebral column. From the viewpoint of the student of equitation, the possible movements of the head and neck are of great importance.

MUSCULAR SYSTEM

For almost every muscle or group of muscles having a certain general action, there is another muscle or group of muscles whose action is the exact opposite. The most important examples are the "extensor" and "flexor" muscles of the legs. A muscle is an "extensor" when its action is to extend a joint and bring the bones into alignment. A muscle is a "flexor" when its action is to bend the joint. Some muscles, if their points of origin and insertion are separated by two or more joints, may act as a flexor of one joint and an extensor of another joint. Except to establish fixation and rigidity of a part, such opposed muscles do not act simultaneously in opposition to each other, but act successively. There are hundreds of muscles in the body and their actions are very complex, but in this text we will consider only the general action of the important muscle groups.

Muscles of the Neck and Shoulder—The long muscles that extend from the region of the shoulder to the sides of the neck and the head are of special interest to the student of equitation for the manner of the movement of the horse is profoundly influenced by their action. With the shoulders fixed, these muscles cause movement of the head and neck, and when the head and neck are fixed by opposing muscular action, these muscles act to advance the shoulder. With the head and neck extended, these muscles are most favorably placed for maximum extension of the shoulder and foreleg with a low and extended action. A high head carriage without shortening of the neck is most favorable for maximum elevation of the shoulder and foreleg, resulting in a higher and shortened stride. Much of the early training of the remount is directly aimed at gaining suppleness and control of the action of this group of muscles.

Muscles of the Back, Loin, and Croup—The triangular space on either side of the spine or the backbone in the region of the back and loins is filled with large muscles. The principal one of this group is the "longissimus dorsi," the longest and largest muscle of the body. It extends from the posterior part of the loin along the back and down between the shoulder and thorax to the last cervical vertebra. These muscles, one on each side, are used extensively when the horse rears or elevates its hindquarters in kicking. Acting singly, the muscles flex the vertebral column laterally. In the thoracic region, this muscular pad bears the weight of the saddle when the horse is ridden and distributes the weight evenly to the supporting ribs. The croup and thighs are made up of groups of powerful muscles which are the chief sources of propelling power.

Fatigue of the Muscles—Fatigue of the muscles follows continued work. This is due primarily to the accumulation of waste products in the muscle cells. As soon as the accumulated waste products are removed by the blood and lymph and a fresh supply of nutrition is brought to the muscles, a feeling of fitness again prevails. Hand rubbing of the legs of the horse is beneficial because the blood and lymph vessels are stimulated to increase activity in the removal of the waste products. It also causes the blood to circulate more freely. Fatigue may also be overcome, in part, by providing a feed of easily digested carbohydrates, which furnishes a maximum of energy.

A green horse (one that is not accustomed to steady work) fatigues much more easily than a hardened horse. This is due to the muscles of the former being softer and possibly carrying an excess of fat. It should be remembered that there is a limit to continued muscular effort, and that harmful fatigue can be avoided only by working the horse at a moderate rate in order to keep the proper balance between the products of muscular activity and the ability of the blood to remove the waste material. An animal should never be worked until exhausted, if for no other reason than that it is not economical.

Appendix IV

Excerpts from *Ecole De Caval*

The following thoughts were expressed by de la Guerinire in his book *Ecole de Caval,* Volume II, Chapter I, entitled "Why Are There So Few Good Riders? The Peculiarities Of A Good Rider." It was written more than two hundred years ago and published in 1733. Many readers will find startling parallels to the confusion and controversy we have to deal with in our times. De la Guerinire wrote:

"The sciences and arts are subject to their own rules and regulations, the study of them serves progress. Riding is seemingly the only art in which practice is enough to learn it. But every practice without the foundation of proper guidelines is an aimless drill and some sort of cheap elegance. Only the layman permits himself to be deluded. Anyway, they are more impressed by the horse than the ability of the rider. It is therefore understandable that one sees nowadays so

few well-trained horses and the imperfect ability of
most riders who think about themselves as good riders.
Without proper guidelines it is also impossible for the
young riders to learn what is right or wrong. Nothing is
then left for them but to imitate others. Unfortunately,
by doing so, the imitation of incorrectness is more obvious than the adoption of correctness. Some try to
imitate such riders who are able to perform with their
horses with utmost accuracy. In doing so, they make
the great mistake of neglecting their seat by continuously giving very visible aids. They mistreat their
horses by shortening the horse's neck and bring the
head behind the perpendicular. In time the horse gets
dull to the rider's legs by tilting the head and brings
one ear lower, mostly the right one. This mistreatment
is the reason for the disobedience of the horse.

"Others try to ride with utmost accuracy but forget
that their idol has great knowledge to judge the possibilities of a green horse. They know that nature has
to give a horse a good conformation. Horses with such
qualities are hard to find. Inexperienced riders who are
left without the proper guidelines will take away from
a good horse the inborn abilities and willingness to
move freely forward.

"Finally, others try to adapt themselves to the so
called good taste of the public, a taste against which
one will seldom rebel. After long and laborious work
they are left only the flattering and fallacious satisfac-
tion of believing they are superior to others.

"The names of the great riding masters are without
doubt connected with the glorious times in riding. Unfortunately only few left guidelines and gave us their
lifework. Of many authors two most greatly admired
are de la Broue and the Duke of Newcastle. Some
French, Italian, and German guidelines are either too
short to be of any help or are written in such a chaotic
manner that they stifle the simple truth. So we are real-

ly left with only the two authors already mentioned. I believe in methodic and correct guidelines. I have therefore explained the most instructive thoughts of both authors in my book. These could also be used as parallels of the guidelines I have written. The books of the two authors are of no help to any rider because they are written in an ill-planned form and with too many repetitions. I hope I was able to avoid this in my book.

"The diffused opinion, that theory has or is of no use for riding will not keep me from affirming that without theory no accomplishied art of riding will exist. Without it every practice is aimless. I admit that theory and practice should not be divorced, because the rider's seat has to play a very important role in the art of riding. It is the practice through which we are able to feel the abilities and possibilities of the horse which makes it possible to bring out from the inability of an untrained horse's body the hidden possibilities and elegance. A clear and sound theory is indispensable to prepare us for the unavoidable complexity in the practice. It instructs us to work on the basis of correct guidelines, instead of working contrary to nature it serves to perfect.

"The practice is nothing more than the in reality transformed theory. For this we need the peculiarities of a good rider: his love for a horse, strength, courage and very great patience.

"All human beings love horses. I think everyone is thankful for the many ways a horse makes itself useful, gives willingly the work we expect from it, and also the pleasure it gives us in so many other ways. A rider who loves not his horse will only bring himself danger. When I mention strength and courage I do not mean brutal and daring riders, but I mean the relaxed strength of the rider which keeps the horse obedient to move relaxed, balanced, and elegant. These peculiarities of a good rider bring him on the way to perfection.

"Difficulties have to be overcome through considerable time by strengthening the horse's muscles. This is the reason many think dressage is useless. Therefore many riders neglect the gymnastic exercises through which every rider can achieve relaxation, balance, obedience and collection. Without these exercises no horse will show good free movements and let the rider sit comfortably, regardless of the use by the rider: fox hunting, jumping, riding intricate figures, or all this together. Therefore it does not make any sense to discuss these unwarranted opinions. Art speaks for itself."

ARENAS FOR DRESSAGE COMPETITIONS

• 1 METER = 3.3 FEET •

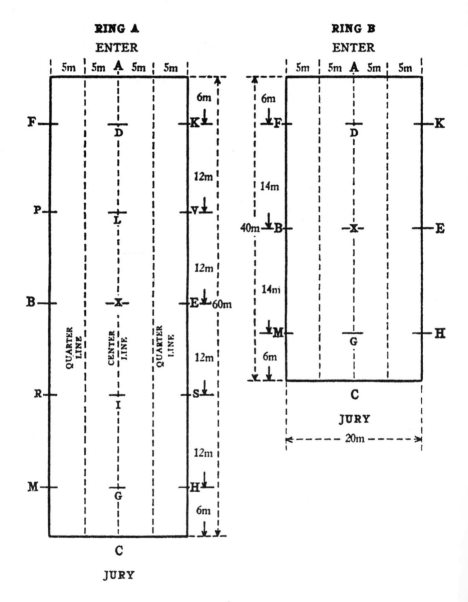

Public to be at least 20m. (66') from all sides of Arena.

Appendix V

Dressage Tests

DRESSAGE TEST A-1 (RING B)

A   Enter ordinary walk.

X   Halt. Salute. Proceed at ordinary walk.

C   Track to the right.

A   Ordinary trot (posting).

K-M   Cross diagonal.

H-F   Cross diagonal strong trot (posting). Then ordinary trot (sitting).

A   Ordinary walk.

E   Halt. Turn on forehand 180° left.

B   Halt. Turn on forehand 180° right. Then ordinary trot (sitting).

C   Circle, tangent to sides developing ordinary canter, right lead.

           On approaching C second time, track to right, ordinary trot (sitting).

M-X-K Cross diagonal. Halt at X. Resume ordinary trot (sitting).

A	Circle, tangent to sides, developing ordinary canter, left lead.
	On approaching A second time, track to left, ordinary trot (posting).
F-X-H	Cross diagonal, strong trot (posting).
H	Ordinary trot (sitting).
C-A	Serpentine width of ring, of three loops.
A	Track to right, ordinary trot (posting).
K-X-M	Strong trot (posting).
M-H	Ordinary trot (sitting).
H-X-F	Strong trot (posting).
F	Ordinary trot (sitting).
A	Turn down middle line.
X	Halt. Salute.
X-C-B-A	Leave ring, free walk, long, but not loose reins. Then jump one obstacle about 2'6".

DRESSAGE TEST A-2 (RING B)

A	Enter ordinary trot (sitting).
X	Halt. Salute. Proceed ordinary trot (sitting).
C	Track to right.
M	Volt.
M-K	Cross diagonal, strong trot (posting).
K-F	Ordinary trot (sitting).
F	Volt.
F-M	Strong trot (posting).
M	Ordinary walk.
H-K	Leg yielding with right leg. At K straighten.
A	Halt. Turn on forehand 180° right, then ordinary walk.
K-H	Leg yielding with left leg. At H straighten.
C	Halt. Then turn on forehand 180° left. Then ordinary trot (sitting).
K	Ordinary canter, left lead.
A	One circle. Then ordinary trot (sitting).

	Track to left.
F-X-H	Cross diagonal.
H	Ordinary canter, right lead.
C	One circle. Then track to right.
M-F	Strong canter.
F-K	Ordinary canter.
K-X-M	Cross diagonal.
M	Simple change of lead, left.
H-K	Strong canter.
K-F	Ordinary canter.
F-X-H	Cross diagonal.
H	Simple change of lead, right.
M	Ordinary trot (sitting).
B	Volt.
F	Halt. Back about 6 feet. Resume ordinary trot (sitting).
A	Down middle line.
G	Halt. Salute.
C-B-A	Leave ring free walk, long but not loose reins. Then jump one obstacle about 2'6".

DRESSAGE TEST A-3 (RING B)

A	Enter ordinary trot (sitting).
X	Halt. Salute. Proceed ordinary trot (posting). At C track to left.
H-X-F	Cross diagonal, strong trot (posting).
F-K	Ordinary trot (sitting).
K-X-M	Cross diagonal, strong trot (posting).
M-H	Ordinary trot (sitting).
K	Ordinary canter, left.
F-X-H	Cross diagonal. Simple change of lead, right at X.
M-X-K	Cross diagonal. Simple change of lead, left at X.
F-M	Strong canter.

M-H	Ordinary canter.
H-K	Strong canter.
K-A	Ordinary canter.
A	Ordinary walk.
B	Halt. Back about 6 feet. Then ordinary trot (sitting).
C	Ordinary walk.
H-K	Leg yielding with left leg, at K straighten.
A	Halt. Turn on forehand 180° right. Then ordinary walk.
K-H	Leg yielding with right leg, at H straighten.
C	Halt. Turn on forehand 180° left. Then ordinary trot (posting).
E-X-B-E	Figure eight, width of ring, changing posting diagonals at center point. Track to left, ordinary trot (sitting).
A	Turn down middle line.
G	Halt. Salute.
G-C-E-A	Leave ring, free walk, long but not loose reins. Then jump one obstacle about 2'6".

DRESSAGE TEST B-1 (RING B)

A	Enter ordinary trot (sitting).
X	Halt. Salute. Proceed ordinary walk.
C	Track to right.
A	Ordinary trot (sitting).
B	Volt.
K-M	Cross diagonal, strong trot (posting).
M-H	Ordinary trot (sitting) with volt at center point C.
H-K	Strong trot (posting).
K-A	Ordinary trot (sitting).
A	Halt. Back about 6 feet, then ordinary trot (sitting).
K-M	Strong trot (posting).

M-H	Ordinary trot (sitting).
H-F	Cross diagonal, strong trot (posting).
F	Ordinary trot (sitting).
A	Ordinary walk.
E	Ordinary canter, right lead.
A	Halt. Turn on haunches 180° right, then walk.
F	Ordinary canter, left lead.
B	Volt.
M	Half volt without change of lead. Return to track at B.
A	Simple change of lead, right.
E	Volt.
H	Half volt without change of lead. Return to track at E.
A	Simple change of lead left.
F-M	Strong canter.
M	Ordinary canter.
H-X-F	Cross diagonal. At X simple change of lead, right.
K-H	Strong canter.
H	Ordinary canter.
M-H-K	Cross diagonal. At X simple change of lead, left.
A	Halt. Turn on haunches 180° left, then ordinary trot (posting).
K-H	Strong trot (posting).
H-M	Ordinary trot (sitting).
M-F	Strong trot (posting).
F	Ordinary trot (sitting).
A	Down middle line.
G	Halt. Salute.
G-C-B-A	Leave ring free walk, long but not loose reins. Then jump two obstacles about 2′6″.

DRESSAGE TEST B-2 (RING B)

A	Enter ordinary trot (posting).
X	Halt. Salute.
X-C-B	Proceed at ordinary walk.
B-A	Ordinary trot (sitting).
A	Volt.
K-M	Cross diagonal.
C	Halt. Back about 6 feet. Proceed ordinary walk.
E-A	Ordinary trot (sitting).
A	Volt.
F-H	Cross diagonal.
C-A	Serpentine of 4 loops starting on the right hand; loops to be half circles with radius from middle line half way to track. Track to left.
A-B-C-E	Ordinary canter, left lead.
E	Volt.
K	Half volt. Without change of lead return to track at 45° angle.
C	Simple change of lead, right.
B	Volt.
F	Half volt. Without change of lead return to track at B.
C	Simple change of lead, left.
H-K	Strong canter.
K-F	Ordinary canter.
F-M	Strong canter.
M-C	Ordinary canter.
C	Ordinary trot (sitting), reins in one hand.
H-F	Cross diagonal, strong trot (posting).
F-A	Ordinary trot (sitting). At A reins in both hands.
A	Halt. Turn on haunches 180° right. Resume ordinary trot (sitting).
F-M	Strong trot (posting).

M-C	Ordinary trot (sitting).
C	Halt. Turn on haunches 180° left. Resume ordinary trot (posting).
A	Turn down middle line.
X	Halt. Salute.
X-C-E-A	Leave ring free walk, long but not loose reins.

DRESSAGE TEST B-3 (RING B)

A	Enter ordinary trot (sitting).
X	Halt. Salute, then ordinary trot (posting).
C	Track to left.
A	Volt.
B	Halt. Then ordinary walk.
C	Halt. Turn on haunches 180° left, proceed ordinary trot (sitting).
B	Volt.
A	Halt. Turn on haunches 180° right, proceed ordinary walk.
B	Halt. Back about 6 feet. Then ordinary trot (sitting).
C	Circle once around, then change through the circle, track to right.
A	Halt. Then ordinary walk.
K	Ordinary canter, right lead.
H	Half volt without change of lead, returning to track at 45° angle.
E	Turn left with counter lead.
X	Halt. Back about 6 feet. Resume canter, left lead, track to left at B.
M	Half volt without change of lead, returning to track at 45° angle.
B	Turn right with counter lead.
X	Halt. Resume ordinary canter, right lead, track to right at E.

M-E	Cross half the ring without change of lead.
A	Simple change of lead, left.
F-E	Cross half the ring without change of lead.
C	Simple change of lead, right.
M-F	Strong canter, reins in one hand.
F-K	Ordinary canter.
K-H	Strong canter, reducing to ordinary trot (sitting) at C. Reins in both hands.
M-K	Cross diagonal, strong trot (posting).
K-F	Ordinary trot (sitting).
F-H	Cross diagonal, strong trot (posting).
C	Ordinary walk.
B	Ordinary trot (sitting).
A	Turn down middle line.
X	Halt. Salute.
X-C-B-A	Leave ring, ordinary walk, long but not loose reins. Then jump two obstacles about 2′6″.

DRESSAGE TEST C-1 (RING B)

A	Enter collected canter, right lead.
G	Halt. Salute. Then collected trot (sitting).
C	Track to right.
F	Half volt, returning to track at B.
K	Half volt, returning to track at E.
C-F	Extended walk.
F	Collected walk.
A	Turn down middle line.
D-B-G	Traversale right to B, then left to G.
G-X	At G, turn on haunches 180° left. Collected walk to X. Turn on haunches 180° right. Resume collected walk.
X-G-C	Return to G, halt. Back 6 steps; advance 6 steps; back 6 steps. Collected trot (sitting). Track to left.

F-X-M	Traversale left to X, then right to M.
M-H	Collected trot (sitting).
H-F	Cross diagonal, extended trot (posting).
F-K	Collected trot (sitting).
K-M	Cross diagonal, extended trot (posting).
M	Collected trot (sitting).
C-A	Serpentine of four loops, width of ring, track to right.
A	Collected walk.
K	Collected canter, right lead.
B	Simple change of lead, left.
A	With counter lead, down middle line.
X	Halt.
X-C	Resume collected canter, right lead, track to left with counter lead.
E	Flying change of lead, left.
E	Reins in one hand.
F-M	Extended canter.
M-H	Collected canter.
H-K	Extended canter.
K	Collected canter, reins in both hands.
B-X-E-B	Figure eight with flying change of lead at center point X. Repeat retaining left lead, track to left.
C	Ordinary trot (sitting).
A	Turn down middle line.
X	Halt. Salute.
X-C-B-A	Leave ring free walk, long but not loose reins. Then jump two obstacles about 3'.

DRESSAGE TEST C-2 (RING B)

A	Enter at collected canter.
G	Halt. Salute. Then strong walk, reins in one hand.
C	Track to right.

M-K	Cross diagonal, extended walk.
K-F	Strong walk.
F-H	Cross diagonal, extended walk.
H-M	Strong trot (sitting).
M-K	Cross diagonal extended trot (posting).
K-F	Strong trot (sitting).
F-H	Cross diagonal extended trot (sitting), reins in both hands.
H-M-B	Collected trot (sitting).
B-X-E-B	Figure of eight across ring, track to right.
A	Collected walk.
K-X	Traversale right.
X-H	Traversale left.
C	Halt. Back 6 steps; strong trot (posting).
M-K	Cross diagonal, at X halt. Then collected trot (sitting).
F-X	Traversale left.
X-M	Traversale right.
C	Halt. Back 6 steps; collected canter left lead.
E	Volt.
F-H	Cross diagonal, simple change of lead, right, at X.
C	Halt. Back 6 steps; collected canter right lead.
B	Volt.
K-M	Cross diagonal, simple change of lead, left, at X.
H-F	Cross diagonal, flying change of lead, right, at X.
K-M	Cross diagonal, flying change of lead, left, at X.
C	Collected (sitting).
E	Collected canter, left lead.
A-C	Serpentine of four loops, without change of lead; track to right in counter lead.
M	Collected trot (sitting).

B	Collected canter, right lead.
A-C	Serpentine of four loops, without change of lead.
H	Collected trot (sitting).
E	Turn right.
X	Strong canter, right lead.
B	Track to right.
K-H	Extended canter.
H	Collected trot (sitting).
B	Turn right.
X	Strong canter, left lead.
E	Track to left.
F-M-C	Extended canter.
C	Strong trot (posting).
H-F	Cross diagonal, change posting diagonal at X.
A	Down middle line, center point.
X	Halt. Salute.
X-C-E-A	Leave ring, extended walk. Then jump two obstacles about 3 ft.

DRESSAGE TEST C-3 (RING B)

A	Enter at collected canter.
X	Halt. Salute. Then collected trot (sitting).
C-B-E-C	Track to right, strong trot (posting).
C-B-K	Collected trot (sitting).
K-M	Cross diagonal, extended trot (posting).
M-H	Collected trot (sitting).
H-E	Shoulder in.
E	Volt.
E-K	Haunches in.
A-X	Shoulder in, left.
X-H	Traversale left.
M-B	Haunches out.
B	Straighten.

K-E	Shoulder in.
E	Volt.
E-H	Haunches in.
C-X	Down middle line, shoulder in, right.
X-K	Traversale, right.
K	Haunches out.
B	Straighten.
B-C-E	Strong trot (posting), reins in one hand.
E	Collected trot (sitting).
A	Down middle line.
X	Halt. Reins in both hands. Back 3 steps then collected canter, left.
C	Track to left.
A	Halt. Turn on haunches 180° left. Then collected canter right.
C	Volt.
B	Simple change of lead, left.
A-X	Counter lead, down middle line, simple change of lead right at X.
C	Track to left with counter lead.
E	Flying change of lead, left.
F-E	Cross half ring, flying change of lead, right at E.
M-E-A	Cross half ring, flying change of lead, left at E.
A-C	Serpentine of four loops, width of ring, with flying change of lead on crossing middle line. Track to right.
C-B-A-H	Strong canter, reins in one hand.
H-M	Collected canter.
M-F	Extended canter.
A-K	Collected trot (sitting).
K-M	Cross diagonal, extended trot (sitting).
M-H	Collected trot (sitting).
H-K	Extended trot (posting).
A	Halt. Reins in both hands. Back 6 steps, collected walk.

B	Extended walk.
C	Collected walk.
E-X-G	Turn left. At X turn left. At G halt. Salute.
G-C-B-A	Leave ring, free walk, long, but not loose reins. Then jump two obstacles about 3 feet.

DRESSAGE TEST D-1 (RING A)

A	Enter collected canter.
X	Halt. Salute, then collected trot (sitting), reins in one hand.
C	Track to right.
M-X-K	Cross diagonal, strong trot (posting).
F-X-H	Cross diagonal, extended trot (posting).
H-C	Collected trot (sitting).
C	Collected canter, right.
M-X-K	Cross diagonal, flying change left at X.
K-F	Collected canter.
F-X-H	Cross diagonal, collected canter, flying change right at X.
H-C	Collected canter.
B	Turn right.
X	Turn right.
G	Halt 8 seconds, then collected trot (sitting), reins in both hands.
C	Turn right.
R	Turn on haunches 180° right at walk. Then collected trot (sitting).
S	Turn on haunches 180° left at walk. Then collected trot (sitting).
M-X	Traversale right.
X-F	Traversale left.
A-C	Turn right. Traversale 7 times, 2 meters (6.6 ft) each side middle line. Terminate movement in manner to take track to left at C.

E	Turn left.
X	Halt. Back 3 steps, advance 6 steps, back 6 steps. Then collected trot (sitting). All without perceptible halt.
B	Track to right.
K-X-M	Cross diagonal, extended trot (sitting).
M-H	Collected trot (sitting).
H-X-F	Cross diagonal, extended trot (sitting).
F-A	Collected trot (sitting).
K	Collected canter, right.
V-X	Traversale right. At X flying change, left.
X-I	Straighten.
I-H	Traversale left.
C	Flying change, right.
M-F	Extended canter.
F	Collected canter.
A-C	Serpentine of ten loops starting on right hand. Flying change of lead on crossing middle line.
C	Track to left, left lead.
H-K	Extended canter.
K	Collected canter.
F-M	Change lead 4 times every 4 strides.
E	Turn left.
X	Turn left.
I	Half pirouette left.
L	Half pirouette right.
X	Collected walk.
G	Halt. Salute.
G-C-E-A	Leave ring extended walk.

DRESSAGE TEST D-2 (RING A)

A	Enter collected canter.
X	Halt. Salute. Then strong trot (posting), reins in one hand.

C	Track to left.
H-X-F	Cross diagonal, extended trot (posting).
F-K	Collected trot (sitting).
K-X-M	Cross diagonal extended trot (posting).
M-E	Collected trot (sitting) reins in both hands.
E	Turn left.
X	Volt to the left, then to the right.
B	Track to the right.
A	Turn down center line.
D-P	Traversale right.
P-S	Traversale left.
S-G	Traversale right.
G-C	Straighten. C track to right, collected walk.
M-X-K	Cross diagonal, extended walk.
A-X	Turn down middle line, collected walk.
X-H	Traversale left.
C	Half-pirouette, right.
V	Turn left.
L	Turn left.
X-M	Promenade right.
C	Half-pirouette, left.
M	Collected trot (sitting).
P	Collected canter, left (false).
E	Collected walk.
H	Turn right.
G	Halt. Back 3 steps, advance 4 steps, back 6 steps, then collected canter right.
M	Track to right.
K-X-M	Cross diagonal, extended canter.
M	Collected canter.
C	Change lead, left.
H-X-F	Cross diagonal 5 times, flying changes every 2 strides.
F	Collected canter.
A	Change lead, right and turn down middle line.
D-P	Traversale right.

P-X	Traversale left.
X-R	Traversale right.
R-G	Traversale left.
C	Track to left.
E-X-B	Figure of eight, retaining left lead.
E	Track to left.
A	Turn down middle line.
L	Pirouette left.
I	Pirouette right.
G	Halt. Salute.
G-C-B-A	Leave ring free walk.

DRESSAGE TEST D-3 (RING A)

A	Enter collected canter.
X	Halt. Salute. Strong trot (posting), reins in one hand.
C	Turn right.
M-K	Cross diagonal.
F-H-B	Cross diagonal, extended trot (posting).
B	Collected trot (sitting).
A	Down middle line.
L	Halt. 8 seconds immobility. Reins in both hands. Collected trot.
X	Turn left.
E	Turn left.
F-E	Traversale left.
E-M	Traversale right.
C	Collected walk.
H-F	Cross diagonal, extended walk.
F-A-X	Collected walk.
X	Volt left, then volt right. Then collected canter, right lead.
C	Turn right.
B	Turn right.

X	Halt. 8 seconds immobility. Then piaffe 10-15 steps. Then collected canter, right lead.
E	Right turn, reins in one hand.
M-F	Serpentine of four loops, 10 feet from track.
F	Reins in both hands.
K-L	Traversale right.
L-I	Straight.
I-M	Traversale right.
M	Flying change.
H-I	Traversale left.
I-L	Straight ahead.
L-F	Traversale left.
F	Flying change.
A	Reins in one hand.
E-C-F	Extended canter.
F-E	Collected canter.
E	Turn right.
X	Halt. Reins in both hands. Back 6 steps, collected walk.
B	Turn left.
C	Halt. Collected canter, left lead.
E	Half-pirouette.
H	Flying change.
B	Half-pirouette.
M	Flying change.
H-A-M	Extended canter, reins in one hand.
M-H	Collected canter.
H-F	Cross diagonal.
X	Flying change.
F	Reins in both hands.
A-C	Serpentine of ten loops; first five with flying change at middle line; last five without change of lead.
C	Turn to left.
H-F	Cross diagonal, 9 times flying change every 2 strides.

K-M	Cross diagonal, 15 times flying change every stride.
C	Down middle line.
I	Pirouette left.
L	Pirouette right.
D	Collected trot.
A-E-X	Passage.
X	Piaffe 10-15 steps. Then passage.
B-P-L-X	Passage.
X	Piaffe 10-15 steps. Then strong trot (sitting), reins in one hand.
C	Left hard.
H-F	Extended trot.
F-K	Collected trot.
K-M	Extended trot.
M-H	Collected trot.
H-K	Extended trot.
K	Collecterd trot, reins in both hands.
A	Down center line.
X	Halt. Salute.

Index